WIDOW BASQUIAT

WIDOW BASQUIAT

Jennifer Clement

First published in Great Britain in 2000 by Payback Press, an
imprint of Canongate Books, 14 High Street, Edinburgh EH1 1TE
Scotland

Published simultaneously in the
United States of America and Canada
in 2001 by Payback Press

10 9 8 7 6 5 4 3 2 1

British Library Cataloguing-in-Publication Data
A catalogue record for this book is available on request from the
British Library

ISBN 1 84195 165 X

Typeset by Hewer Text Ltd, Edinburgh.
Printed and bound by WS Bookwell, Finland

For Suzanne

'Suzanne, you are a cartoon.'
Jean-Michel Basquiat

SHE IS THIS GIRL

She always keeps her heroin inside her bee-hive hair-do. The white powder hidden in the tease and spit. The cops can't find it. The drug addicts can't find it. Suzanne holds her head high. She's carrying a world without corners. She's holding up the sky. Slight enough to go down chimneys, Suzanne looks like a little girl dressed up in her mother's clothes. She wears 'Love-That-Red' lipstick by Revlon and has blue-black hair and white skin. She closes up all the buttons in her shirt.

Suzanne can knit, ice skate, sing, read palms and smoke dozens of cigarettes to keep warm inside. Little girls love her because she tells them, 'Hey, little missy, I can hear your heart.' They think she's a music box.

When Suzanne was ten years old her mother said, 'let's have a tea party.' They sat together at the kitchen table. It was the first time Suzanne had ever drunk tea. She put four teaspoons of sugar in it. She said 'it's too cold.'

Her mother said, 'I'll only tell you this once so mark my words.'

'I broke the rocking horse,' Suzanne said.

'You of all my children were made like an angel. But you want to look over the edge to hell. Always know where that line is and never cross it. And here are nine kisses,' her mother continued, 'for every year of your life.'

While she kissed her again and again on the forehead, Suzanne wished her mother wore lipstick so that the kisses would be painted on and everyone would know.

She wanted to say, 'But I'm ten really.'

WORN WITH SOUNDS

Suzanne's mother claims to be a witch. She puts her head down, claps her hands and concentrates. She calls this 'cursing people'. Once a man who owned a television store in town asked her, 'Who winds you up in the morning?' That night his store burned down. But she can't stop Suzanne's father from beating up the kids.

'He's an Arab,' she says, 'what can I do? Curses don't get into those black eyes.'

Suzanne has a scar on her forehead from when he threw her down the stairs. It is shaped like the number five.

Her childhood is worn with sounds: chairs against walls; 'you good for nothing punk!'; the snake belly-slide of a belt, the soft drum sound of a three-year-old's head against a wall; 'you good for nothing punk'; tears that mix with *Captain Crunch* cereal; 'you good for nothing punk'; a hand the size of a maple leaf slapping; the twist and crack of arms and wrists; 'walk on tip-toe, shhh', whisper. 'He's home.'

'Don't worry, honey,' Suzanne's mother says to Suzanne. 'One day you'll set the world on fire.'

PAPER DRESSES

Four draft dodgers and Suzanne sit at the kitchen table. Suzanne's mother is known in the underground of draft dodgers so men come to Orangeville, Ontario, Canada to sit at this table dressed in love beads and leather bracelets to ask Suzanne where they can get some pot.
Suzanne giggles and pulls some plastic bags filled with marijuana out of her white knee-high boots.

Suzanne wears paper dresses and maxi-coats. One draft dodger likes to tease her by burning cigarette holes in her dresses. Another one tells her if the war ever ends he's going to come back and marry her.

'I'll never marry anyone,' Suzanne says. 'No man is big enough for my arms.'

I had very hard working parents. My father had a painting/construction business that at its height employed forty men. My mother had a nursery school in our house. She took all children. She did not close the door to any child. There were normal, retarded, autistic, blind and crippled children. There was nowhere for these disabled children to go. My mother was a real radical. During the Vietnam War she took in

4

American draft dodgers. I was too young to know what this meant. These hippies with long hair and beards would just appear at the dinner table. During those Vietnam years my mother must have taken care of forty of these young men. My father was against this and I heard them fighting over it. My father thought they were cowards. My mother thought they were pacifists and she thought that they were too young. My mother became known in the underground of draft dodgers and boys from all over America came, knowing they would get food and a roof over their heads. They would sleep on the living room floor.

My father was intelligent and hard working. He taught himself everything. He drove a big Cadillac so that we would be like the children of the doctors and lawyers. However, he was domineering and violent. He believed that we would respect him if we feared him. We feared him.

ONLY ONE
CHROMOSOME IS MISSING

Suzanne walks down the steps from her bedroom. In the hall her mother is feeding a mentally retarded child who is tied with a rope to a chair. The little boy is tied up so he will not mutilate himself. He scratches his face until it bleeds. The doorbell rings and two more children with Down's Syndrome arrive. This is Suzanne's mother's latest business venture. There are no facilities for abnormal children in Orangeville.

Suzanne thinks, 'These are the children that need to go to the doll hospital.'

For three years the house shelters three or four of these children a day. Their hands get washed, their backs get rubbed, they break things they find. But this house doesn't shelter black and blue children.

The black and blue children are thinking about running away. They think, 'We don't fit in this house.'

Suzanne loves one of the retarded kids called Sammy. Sammy is a six year old Black girl. Suzanne knows only one chromosome is missing in her beautiful little face. Suzanne braids Sammy's hair and buys her candy.

Suzanne makes her dresses that she copies out of Vogue magazine and she teaches Sammy to count to five.

One day Suzanne and Sammy are sitting in the garden when Suzanne's mother comes outside, 'Now you girls be careful, you're going to turn your skin too dark,' she says.

Once she gave Suzanne a whole case of bleaching skin cream. 'If you think about it hard enough,' Suzanne's mother says, 'you can change the way you look.'

'If you think about it hard enough,' Suzanne tells Sammy, 'you can make that chromosome grow in you.' Sammy looks straight at the sun. She can do that and not even squint or blink.

THE MAGIC HORSETAIL

Suzanne's mother has a magic horsetail. Out of a short, carved, ivory stick hangs a white horse's tail. It was given to her by her great aunt for luck when she was little, growing up in England. She took it with her to Beirut where she was a British naval officer. It was here that she met Suzanne's father. Together they moved to Canada as Palestinian refugees. The horsetail has always been with her.

Suzanne braids the horsetail, shakes it around. 'Make lots of wishes with it, Suzy,' Suzanne's mother says.

'Did you make wishes with it?' Suzanne asks.

'Oh, millions and millions. But I don't believe in making wishes.'

Suzanne's mother always tells lies. She says she saw a woman in Beirut who had transparent skin. She says there are forty-two ways to cut an apple. She says she's seen the vaults with the gold reserves of England. She says the Earth has two moons. She says she has eaten sheep eyes, ant larvae and raw eggs because she was working as a spy.

She tells Suzanne, 'You have your father's barbaric blood. You are genetically more Arab than your brothers and sisters. You will always have problems with hysteria, rage and jealousy.'

Every time Suzanne thinks about her mother's sulphur-blue eyes it rains.

SKELETON

Suzanne has always made a wish to herself. But it is not really a wish because it is going to happen no matter what. She's going to leave. She's known this ever since she could look in the mirror at her face.

When she was six, she walked alone around the block for the first time and it felt good. After that, she did it everyday always walking a little bit farther. In the winter, she'd walk and walk around the house looking for cobwebs which she would eat to make her strong.

Suzanne knows her skeleton. She knows where every bone is and which one hurts most. She knows the bruise from falling on ice is different from a bruise from a belt. She has studied the length of her tibia and the width of her femur. The pull of hair from the nape of the neck is different from the pull of hair from the forehead. She has learned the swivel and turn from a hand that can cover her whole face.

At night Suzanne lies in her bed listening to her father play trick-track with his friends who have also come to Canada as Palestinian refugees. Sometimes, she sneaks down, watches them and her father pulls her out of the shadows.

He strokes her hair and gives her a taste of beer with his finger.

Sometimes I would jump on his back to stop him and I would get thrown across the room. Once when I was five he threw me down the stairs and I hit my head on a heater. I still have the scar on my forehead. He often threw us across the room and we would hit furniture or walls. He would also pick up furniture and throw it at us or break it.

WHAT FURNITURE
FEELS LIKE

A chair feels like a slap.

A table feels like a kick.

A lamp feels like a punch.

A door feels like a shove, but it can be opened.

AND A LIST
OF GOOD EXCUSES

'I fell down the stairs.'

'My brother punched me.'

'I crashed into a tree on my bike.'

'The door slammed in my face.'

'I slipped on the ice.'

'I don't remember.'

'My doll's hand scratched me.'

'The rain fell hard.'

YOU CAN ALWAYS COME BACK

'I know you're going to leave. One day you'll figure it out and leave,' Suzanne's mother says.

'Yes, I know, Mum,' Suzanne answers.

'Well, what have I taught you? What did I fill you up with? You know Suzy, there's a big, bad wolf out there just waiting to eat you up. You can leave but you can always come back. You can live here again. Life can be a circle, not just a line. And don't chew gum ever, Suzy. No lady ever chews gum.'

THE RAINBOW IS HERE

Suzanne's father isn't going to hit her anymore because she's menstruating. She told him, 'I'm a woman now. I'm bleeding now. You can't touch me anymore.'

The house is full of the smell of paint and paint thinners that Suzanne's father mixes up in the basement for his house painting company. The smells fill up the house. Suzanne can tell by now if he's mixing blue or red or yellow. The smell sticks to everybody's skin. It stings Suzanne's mother's eyes. It burns her brothers' and sisters' skin. It makes some of the retarded children faint. Sammy learns to cross her eyes. Suzanne giggles.

Sometimes, Suzanne goes down to the basement while her father is mixing the paint and they giggle together. The fumes are so strong they feel as if they are on a merry-go-round. Suzanne looks into the vat of cobalt blue and thinks she could swim in there. But she just dips her fingers in and they feel so cool.

The grass around the house turns yellow and two cats die from the fumes. Children stop coming to play. The mailman tells people he saw red vapor coming out of the windows. At school the teachers complain that these children are always coming to school with their clothes on inside out.

Suzanne's mother says, 'children, you don't need to be going and leaving and looking for a rainbow. The rainbow is here.'

FEEL GRAY, MUST EXIT

It's easy. You sell everything you own and buy a ticket. Even if you have no place to go, some words have to sing inside. Suzanne has the magic words; they are going to turn her into a bright flag, they are going to make her measure the length of her arms. The words are: Seville Hotel, New York City. It's easy. You sell everything you own.

'Don't cry over anything that can't cry over you,' Suzanne's mother says.

Suzanne has a garage sale. She makes a big sign: FEEL GRAY, MUST EXIT. She sells everything and only keeps two pairs of pants and two T-shirts that she dyes gray in the bathtub.

Her mother buys her toothbrush for one dollar. Her sister buys her birth control pills and Iggy Pop records. Her father says, 'You'll be back.'

Suzanne says, 'Maybe,' and thinks, 'if you'd never hit me, I wouldn't know my skeleton.'

17

THOUGHTS ON A BUS TRIP

There are no footsteps, but you're moving. What is the distance between? Outside the trees move, the houses move. Inside everything is still. The woman in the back is weeping. She wipes her face with her sleeve. The smell of diesel is the smell of movement. Suzanne is sitting with her feet together, her knees together, her hands together, very prim as if waiting for a concert to begin.

Her mother kissed her forehead at the station, 'Be careful, Suzy,' she said. 'Everybody is hungry.' Her brothers and sisters gave her a card. It says, "Suzy Q we love you.' Her father gave her twenty dollars. 'Call us,' he said.

Suzanne sits still, so skinny, knowing the size of her bones. Knowing how to cover bruises with make-up. Knowing how to disappear. She thinks about Sammy, who came and left so quickly, who sucked the salt out of her fingers. She remembers the day Sammy learned to say 'ouch'. And that was all she would say forever after, 'ouch, ouch, ouch,' like a little song.

Suzanne came home from school one day and Sammy wasn't there anymore. 'You know how these kids are,

Suzy,' Suzanne's mother said. 'They just kind of come and go. She was sweet, though.'

You can't get your arms to stop making circles in the air if you never say goodbye.

But the reason I decided to go to New York was because I had seen Iggy Pop and I thought I had seen God. And because I had sent to Interview *magazine for Rene Ricard's first book of poetry* 'The Blue Book'. *I had never sent for anything before but something told me to do this. I had read that book over and over again like a Bible. I realized that a book can reach out and embrace you like an arm and make you walk away from everything you thought you understood.*

THE SEVILLE HOTEL

It is Valentine's Day 1980. The shop windows are filled with red hearts and paper lace. 'I'm going to New York City,' Suzanne told the draft dodgers when they asked, 'Little lady, what are you going to be when you grow up?'

'And,' Suzanne continued, 'I'm going to be famous and eat artichokes.'

'Go to the Seville Hotel,' they said.

THE WELCOMING SPEECH

There are three middle-aged prostitutes in the lobby of the Seville Hotel.

'What's gunna ruin you, girlie?' the one in the blue dress asks.

'What do you mean?' Suzanne answers.

'What she said,' the one in the yellow dress interrupts. 'What's going to ruin you? A man? A job? No job, no man? Your babies? What?'

'A man's gonna ruin her, for sure,' the one in the red dress says. 'Let me tell you, everybody gets ruined by something – even if you're a queen in a castle – something's gonna say, you're mine.'

It was February 14th, Valentine's Day, 1980. I went straight to the Seville Hotel. The first night a prostitute was murdered by the infamous 'Slasher.' It was terrible. There were cops everywhere and the women who were staying at the hotel were moaning and screaming and cussing at the police officers. I was so frightened that I moved out to the Martha Washington Hotel on 29th and

Madison, which was only for women. No men were even allowed in the lobby.

I found Rene Ricard's number in the phone book and I used to call him and we would discuss philosophical things and I would tell him how brilliant I thought he was and read him my own poetry. It never occurred to me that he would not speak to a stranger. He would talk to me for hours. He was very kind. I never told him my name, though, and he never asked. This special telephone friendship lasted for several weeks.

THE RITZ'S CIGARETTE GIRL

Suzanne wears black, elbow length gloves, a short pearl necklace, fish-net stockings and a short skirt with a crinoline underneath. She wears white pancake make-up, thick black eyeliner and red lipstick.

She smells like lemon soap and coffee. She has a red wood cigarette box with compartments. As Suzanne walks around the Ritz nightclub she sing-songs in her sparrow-voice, 'Cigarettes, cigars, lifesavers, joints. Cigarettes, cigars, lifesavers, joints.' She makes a lot of money and rents an apartment on the Lower East Side.

Leroy Neiman, the illustrator from *Playboy*, wants to sketch her. All the young Puerto Rican boys want to go out with her. And the lesbians, the ones who wear Chanel No.5, want to take her home.

She sucks on lifesavers all night. Green, red, yellow, orange. Some people put tips inside her gloves. The owner of the Ritz tells her he loves her and wants to put a hole in her heart. Suzanne quits this job. She tells the owner she can't breath deeply anymore. She gives him her gloves filled with rice.

A week after arriving in New York I was hired as a waitress at Max's Kansas City. It was a very hip place at night like CBGB's. These two places had all the cool bands. I worked in the day and the customers were mostly business people from the offices in the area. When the manager left to manage the Ritz, she took me with her as a cigarette girl. I got fired for selling joints, but it was really because I had been having an affair with one of the owners. Soon I got a job at Night Birds as a bartender.

I did not know anything about being a bartender so I went to a bookstore and bought a book on mixing drinks. I learned all those different drinks and all their names by heart. I became an expert at this by practicing with water at home and pretending to have all the ingredients. However, I didn't really need to know all this since Night Birds was a very dark, seedy bar where taxi drivers stopped by in the afternoon for a beer, and where a few alcoholic men hung out all day. The bar was so dark it always felt like night in there, so it attracted people who did not like day light.

Looking back, it was the perfect place to meet Jean because he liked the night and never liked the day.

ONE FACE

Even though one year has passed, downtown New York is still covered with one face that is marked "MISSING" and "Child last seen going to school bus stop, wearing black pilot-type cap, blue corduroy jacket, blue pants, blue sneakers and carrying blue bag".

On light poles, telephone booths, in shop windows, along the walls of buildings, and in subway stations a small boy's face on a pasted poster looks out. His face is also hidden behind layers of old rock concert posters and advertisements. His name is Etan Patz:

> Age at disappearance: 6
> Date of birth: 10/9/1972
> Date of last contact: 5/25/1979
> Race: White
> Gender: Male
> Height: 3' 04"
> Weight: 50 lbs
> Eyes; Blue
> Hair: Blonde
> Missing from: New York, NY

He has been missing for one hour, one day, one week, one month, one year. His mother is quoted in the newspapers,

"It was the first time I let him walk to the bus stop alone. It was the first time I let him. I never let him go alone before. It was the first time I let him walk to the bus stop alone. It was the first time I let him walk to the bus stop alone."

The graffiti artists never painted on his face.

I don't think he was ever found, but we all thought about him.

SUZANNE MEETS JEAN-MICHEL AT NIGHT BIRDS

Jean-Michel has found Suzanne like a small box, an old coat, a penny on a sidewalk, found a little boy-girl like him. He also knows his skeleton. When he was hit by a car as a child his mother gave him *Gray's Anatomy* to read in the hospital. He willed his bones whole. He knows what makes an arm bend to strike, what bones can be crushed and what bones carry him across the street. He knows his boneless shadow that disappears in Summer. He is in a band called 'Gray'. The band plays instruments hiding in boxes.

Jean-Michel wears a big, long overcoat. He stands away from the bar and comes in everyday to watch Suzanne. She reads *Nausea* by Sartre behind the bar. This is an old man, taxi-driver bar. Cigar-smoke dark. Suzanne looks like a boy except for her red lips. She is a shoe-shine boy with a black cap on her head and big shoes. She asks the customers in her honey, twelve-year-old voice, 'Mister, sir, will that be a double or single?'

Jean-Michel watches Suzanne for two months. He never speaks to her. He leans against the juke box at the back of the room, smokes cigarettes and plays Eartha Kitt's song, 'My Heart Belongs to Daddy,' over and over again. He has very short hair with long dread locks in the back. He is twenty years old, slender and tall, but child-like. There is a thickness about him from his excessive use of marijuana. Suzanne thinks, 'If he falls on me he will be so heavy.'

He only orders the best. Every four days he puts a pile of pennies, nickles and dimes on the bar and orders a Remy. Suzanne knows he will always want what is expensive.

He tells Suzanne, 'You're a pretty one.'

The third or fourth or fifth thing Suzanne tells Jean-Michel is, 'High heels are a plot against women, they throw our spines out and stop us from standing on the ground.'

I always called Jean-Michel Jean.

A GUN IN A PAPER BAG

Jean-Michel comes into the bar everyday. He reads Suzanne his poems from his 'Black and White Notebooks'. He calls her 'Venus'. He tells her he is thinking about her feet, thinking that they are always on the ground. He wants to touch her feet. He tells her to take off her shoes and walk with him in the street.

One day the owner of Night Birds, a Chinese man, shows Suzanne a brown paper bag with a gun in it. 'Why don't you have a nice, white boyfriend?' he asks.

Jean-Michel moves into Suzanne's apartment. He brings only a broken radio and a tin can full of crayons. Kids' stuff.

I had to quit working at Night Birds when the owner caught me and Jean kissing at the bar. He said he would never let his daughter do what I was doing and that I should look for a white boy. Then he showed me a gun he had hidden in a brown paper bag and that really frightened me.

Even though he'd been hanging out at the bar for a few months staring at me, I had only known Jean for a few days,

29

when I let him move into my apartment. He said that it would only be for a while, but from then on we could never stay away from each other.

JEAN-MICHEL BASQUIAT

He smells of leather, oil paint, tobacco, marijuana and the faint, metallic smell of cocaine. He wears handmade wool sweaters and long Mexican ponchos. He never walks in a straight line. He zigzags wherever he is going. Suzanne follows behind him. She feel like a Japanese woman.

Jean-Michel can never get a taxi to stop for him. Not even later when he wears an Armani suit and has five thousand dollars in his pocket. Jean-Michel hides behind a car and Suzanne hails the taxis.

He has the scar of a knife wound on his buttocks. He says his mother is in an insane asylum and that his whole world spins around her.

He moves in with Suzanne.

Jean-Michel brushes Suzanne's hair for hours. He paints or draws. He snorts some coke. He picks up boys or girls at the Mudd Club and disappears for days. He looks at girlie magazines and masturbates. Jean-Michel likes to spit into Suzanne's mouth.

Suzanne and Jean-Michel have terrible fights because only Suzanne is earning money. One day Jean-Michel says, 'Fine, I'll get a job.' He goes to work as an electrician's assistant at the apartment of a rich, white woman. Suzanne is so proud of him she makes him a special dinner.

When Jean-Michel gets back home he is furious, clapping his hands together. 'That white bitch looked at me as if I were a worker!' he says. Jean-Michel throws Suzanne's dinner into the garbage and does some coke. Suzanne locks herself in the closet.

It was clear that his sexual interest was not monochromatic. It did not rely on visual stimulation, such as a pretty girl. It was a very rich multi-chromatic sexuality. He was attracted to people for all different reasons. They could be boys, girls, thin, fat, pretty, ugly. It was, I think, driven by intelligence. He was attracted to intelligence more than anything and to pain. He was very attracted to people who silently bore some sort of inner pain as he did and he loved people who were one-of-a-kind, people who had a unique vision of things.

IN THE CLOSET

In the closet there are two dead spiders. Clothes rolled up on the floor mixed up with shoes. There is a pair of ice skates. The blades are still sharp. Her face rests inside the hem of a winter coat. She can hear Jean-Michel moving around in the kitchen. His shadow moves around beneath the closet door. His shadow touches her hands and feet. The front door slams shut.

Over the stove Jean-Michel has painted faces of little girls crying. He has written in huge block letters: TEARS CUT THEIR CHEEKS.

CADILLAC MOON

With acrylic on canvas Jean-Michel paints a Cadillac and a moon. The letter 'S' appears on some paintings – placed here and there like a small worm or snake. 'S' is for Suzanne, like a tattoo. He paints, pauses, picks up a book or magazine and when he finds a word or sentence that he likes he paints it on the board or canvas.

There are codes: The crown is the logo from the t.v. show 'The Little Rascals'. He mixes Spanish and English. One painting is of Suzanne, painted like a stick-figure holding a box that says, 'FOOD'. Beside her Jean-Michel paints himself carrying a box that says, 'SAL'. *Sal* is Spanish for 'salt' – he says he is a 'Mammy' salt shaker.

He paints kings wearing black crowns covered in tar and feathers. He paints a simple square house with a triangle roof that has an 'S' inside, 'Because, Suzanne, you are my home.'

On one painting he writes, 'Jimmy Best on his back to the suckerpunch of his childhood files,' because he hears a hobo say this on television.

He writes 'TAR' everywhere in thick dark strokes because, 'I sometimes feel as black as tar.'

He knows what it is to have a knife thrown at him. He knows what it is like to be tied up and fed like an animal. He knows the sound of a slap against his cheek and what blood tastes like. He hates the sound of a key in a lock, a door opening, the first step inside.

For a year or so before I met Jean he had called himself, "SAMO". He had painted some graffiti on the walls around New York City signing that name everywhere. Sometimes he'd run into people who still called him that. It was his street name. He dropped it when he no longer wanted to be part of the streets and subways.

ARROZ CON POLLO

They are skeletons – naked inside and naked outside. They sit down to eat naked. Jean-Michel has made his favorite dish, 'arroz con pollo'. His Puerto Rican mother taught him to make it. Suzanne is white; she holds her left breast with her right hand – her other hand holds a fork. Across the table Jean-Michel is black. He wears a red Mexican *charro* hat as he gives Suzanne a plate of steaming chicken. Beside Suzanne is the word 'TAR'. They can see the inside of each others' bodies. Jean-Michel can see Suzanne's teeth and an almond-shaped vagina. Suzanne can see his ribs and shoulder joints. This is a painting: *Arroz con Pollo*, 1981, acrylic and oil paint-stick on canvas, 68 x 84.

One of the hardest things to describe about Jean is his elegance. There was something so beautiful about the way he moved and spoke. This partly had to do with his drug use that kept him very slim and child-like. But it was innate also. I was also very slim and waif-like. We looked twelve years old.

What most people don't understand about Jean-Michel is that his crazy behavior had nothing to do with being an 'enfant terrible'. Everything he did was an attack on racism and I loved him for this.

I also understood racism. My mother tried to get me to bleach my skin. She never wanted me to go out in the sun. She said I was too 'Arab looking'.

I remember that in high school I wanted to play the part of Dorothy in The Wizard of Oz. *I practiced singing the songs for weeks and my voice was the best in the school. They gave the part to another girl because they said my skin was too dark. I remember that I came home and wept. My mother said, 'Suzy, well, they're right.'*

NO BLACK MEN IN MUSEUMS

One Thursday in 1982, Jean-Michel tells Suzanne to stand up and walk, they are going to the MoMA. He tells Suzanne to wear his clothes. She ties his pants around her waist with a rope. His sweater hangs down to her knees.

At the museum Jean-Michel takes a bottle of water out of his coat and walks through the halls sprinkling the water here and there around him. 'I'd piss like a dog if I could,' he says, as they wander past paintings by Pollock, Picasso, Kline and Braque. Suzanne does not even ask what he is doing. She knows this is one of his voodoo tricks.

'There are no black men in museums,' he says. 'Try counting . . .'

Suzanne cannot find even one.

'This is another white man's cotton plantation,' he explains.

When they get back home Jean-Michel puts on a Charlie Parker tape and tells Suzanne to be very quiet.

It begins to rain outside, a slow, dark rain that will not stop for three days.

Jean-Michel paints, *St. Joe Louis Surrounded by Snakes*. It shows the boxer slumped down after a fight, surrounded by a group of sinister-looking white men. Joe Louis is painted with a halo over his head and the paint drips from his name like blood falling down the canvas.

I realized that he must have been to the MoMA millions of times. I had no idea. I never knew when he went. He never mentioned it to me. I know that his mother had taken him to museums. Jean knew every inch of that museum, every painting, every room. I was astonished at his knowledge and intelligence and at how twisted and unexpected his observations could be.

I remember he had a book on Renoir that he loved. Once I asked him why and he said, "because they are so violent." I argued with him and said that he was wrong, that the paintings showed placid, French country life. He said I was stupid. He opened the book and showed me the painting of Mademoiselle Romaine Lacaux.

'Those red flowers,' he said, 'are blood in her hands.' Then he showed me, The Sisleys *and said, 'You can just tell he hates her.' Finally, he opened a page at* The Odalisque – *the one of the harem woman – and Jean said, 'Look, she is about to fart.'*

His favorite painters were Kline and Twombly, especially Twombly. Jean said that Twombly taught him that he could scratch things out on the canvas. And, of course, he loved comic books, which were a great inspiration to him.

It made me so happy that he had taken me with him to the MoMA to do his spell with the water. It was really quite funny watching him sprinkle water everywhere, making sure the guards weren't watching and looking around and up at the ceiling to see if any cameras were on him. He did not think it was funny, though. Jean did it with great seriousness like a priest.

SPLEEN

Jean-Michel has a long scar that extends from his chest to his stomach. When he was eight years old he was hit by a car and had to have his spleen removed. At the hospital, his mother, Matilde, brought him *Gray's Anatomy* to read. He memorized the whole book: tibia, femur, aorta, oral cavity, pharynx, digital nerve, optic chiasm . . .

At the hospital, Matilde touched her son's scar, 'The doctor's say you can live without a spleen. The spleen is an archaic organ.'

Jean-Michel adores Matilde who lives in an asylum outside New York City. Her illness began when Jean-Michel was a young teenager. She would sit for hours and try to imitate the whistling of birds. She got rid of everything in the house that could break.

Jean-Michel visits his mother once a month. He takes his drawings and paintings to show her. Matilde looks at them and says, 'You are moving very fast.'

Jean was particularly close to his youngest sister Jeanine.

Jeanine was very sweet and naive and dressed in white frilly blouses and tartan skirts. Jean's father didn't want Jean to give the girl any money. But when Jeanine came over, Jean would hide 100 dollar bills in the pages of books and give the books to Jeanine as presents.

I was never invited by Jean's father to go to his home, even though I was one of the closest people to Jean. He never expressed an interest in getting to know me. I was always polite and respectful toward Gerard but he always gave me that feeling that I was a 'one night stand' or a casual girlfriend.

Jean he told me that when he was fourteen the family moved to Puerto Rico. Jean ran away and lived with a disc jockey who worked for a local radio station and he told me that this was his first homosexual relationship. He lived in Puerto Rico for about two years and spoke good Spanish. Soon after they moved back to Brooklyn Jean left home for good. He told me he lived on benches in Washington Square Park and on friends' couches.

TU ERES BLANCA COMO EL ARROZ

Some days Jean-Michel wakes up in the morning and can only speak in Spanish: *Si. Si. Leche. Arroz. El niño come platanos. La niña tiene canicas. Tu eres blanca como el arroz. Mi nombre es Juan.*

Some days Jean would wake up and just speak Spanish. I understood very little. He'd go on and on for hours conjuring up everything he could remember like a song in his head. The presence of his mother was with him and he was with her in the words.

FIRST SALE

Suzanne loves polka dots. She is dressed in a wide, polka dot skirt. She and Jean-Michel do a couple of lines of coke and go to the Mudd Club, Tier 3, Club 57, Studio 54, The Roxy or the Continental. Jean-Michel is dressed in big, baggy pants with paint all over them and a big T-shirt and shoes that are way too big. Sometimes they go out and see the Contortions (who later becomes James White and the Blacks), the Lounge Lizards, DNA, Arto Lindsay or Kid Creole and the Coconuts.

Jean-Michel sells his first painting to Deborah Harry from Blondie for 200 dollars and spends the money on one expensive dinner with Suzanne. He leaves a fifty dollar tip.

When he could, he always left enormous tips. He loved to shock, even shock with generosity. It was like punching someone.

LOLLIPOP GIRLS

Suzanne is waitressing at Bini-Bon Restaurant. One Friday night she comes home and finds Jean-Michel doing coke with three white girls dressed up in 40's dresses, false eyelashes, and high heels and looking like fluttering dragonflies.

'We're celebrating' Jean-Michel says. The girls giggle. 'Annina Nosei is going to represent me.' He picks up a knife off of the kitchen table and carves an 'S' into Suzanne's wood floor.

'We are going to be rich just like I told you,' Jean-Michel says laughing. The girls laugh also. Suzanne takes her waitressing tips out of her pocket and throws them at Jean-Michel.

'Here,' she says. 'Get some more coke for you and the girls.'

Jean-Michel leaves the apartment with the three lollipop girls skipping behind him and doesn't return for three days. Later someone tells Suzanne that Jean-Michel was seen at the Mudd Club with a Puerto Rican boy.

When I first moved to New York I was a cigarette girl at the Ritz. Even when I left this job I kept my red wooden cigarette box. One day Jean found it and, thinking it was just a piece of wood or something, he did a painting on it. He painted a face with a crown and the word AARON on it. I was very angry at the time. But I later sold it to Annina Nosei for one thousand dollars.

46

BACK TO CANADA

Too much furniture. Nowhere to move without poking your thigh or hip into a pointed corner of some table, counter or chair. There is some room to sit on the stairs around the piles of magazines and un-ironed clothes.

Suzanne's mother tries on Suzanne's Jackie-O sunglasses. 'These are nice, Suzy' her mother says. Her mother gets up and walks to the kitchen counter. She takes out five dollars from a box of crackers.

'Here, I've been saving these for you,' she says handing the money to Suzanne. 'Nobody likes crackers in this house, so they were safe,' she laughs.

'You know, ' she continues, 'I still think of you as an ice skater. You could still do it, you know. Can I keep these sunglasses?'

'Not this time, Mother,' Suzanne says. 'Jean-Michel likes them a lot and I bought them at a thrift shop.'

'I understand, Suzy,' her mother says. 'Nothing is for keeps, though, remember that.'

BINI-BON RESTAURANT

While Suzanne is in Canada, the boy who is covering her waitressing shifts at Bini-Bons is killed with a knife by Jack Henry Abbott, the man Norman Mailer wrote about in *The Belly of the Beast*. This man has been living in the halfway houses near the Bowery.

Jean-Michel sees the larvae-white paint, the outline of the body drawn by police on the sidewalk.

It takes twenty minutes and forty two seconds for Jean-Michel to run home and call Suzanne in Canada. 'Come home,' he cries. 'It could have been you.'

On the airplane back to New York Suzanne knows that her mother has stolen her sunglasses.

LESSONS ON
HOW TO BE A WOMAN

Jean-Michel gets a hold of a big piece of opium. He smokes it with Suzanne but decides that the best way to do the drug is to put it in the refrigerator, break off small pieces, roll it into a ball and stick it up their rectums. So this is what they do. They lie naked on the floor for days.

One morning Jean-Michel says that an art critic is going to come over and interview him. There is a knock and Jean-Michel, who is naked, answers the door.

Rene Ricard enters the apartment. He says, 'Not only are you the greatest artist I have ever seen, you have the most beautiful penis I have ever seen.' After this meeting, Ricard wrote the 'Radiant Child' article for *Artforum*.

Ricard hires Suzanne as his secretary to transcribe his poetry. Suzanne tells him that she is the girl that used to call him up.

He says, 'of course you were.'

Rene Ricard writes on matchbooks, wrappers and bits of toilet paper. Every week he gives these scraps to Suzanne in a plastic zip-lock bag. He tells her to type everything on a page in any order.

Rene Ricard teaches Suzanne how to behave on the street, how to behave with the young black and Puerto Rican boys and the 'stick-up' kids. Suzanne and Ricard have the same taste in men and he teaches her how to have them in her house and not get robbed. He teaches her how to move and what to say and what not to say. He tells her never to allow them to bring their guns into the bedroom and, if something goes wrong, her best defense is to act as vulnerable, weak and passive as she can. He says never to act tough like a Black girl or they will kill her in a minute.

Rene Ricard says he is going to teach Suzanne how to be feminine, how to be a star. He explains that when she walks into a party, club or art opening, she must never look at anyone but fix her eyes on a point across the room and walk toward it. Above all, though, he tells her to study drag queens because only they know how to act like women.

DOWNTOWN SOCIETY

They dress in long, black waistcoats and walk down 3rd Avenue carrying black and silver walking sticks. At night they wear a top hat. They carry their cigarettes in thin silver cigarette cases. They live without electricity and only use candle light. They have no appliances or even a telephone. Sometimes they perform songs at the new, hip restaurants in Alphabet City and places like 'Evelyn's'. They sing, 'Tea for Two' and 'My Bonnie Lies Over the Ocean' in an acappella harmony. They also paint paintings from a specific time period in the manner of a particular artist and sign them 'McDermott and McGough', followed by the appropriate date: 1789, 1899, 1942, etc.

Vicky is a little frail girl who stutters when she speaks. She deals heroin on 1st street. She has read everything and can quote Dostoevsky.

Lili Dones designs menus for restaurants in the East Village as well as eccentric greeting cards. She wears "Marilyn Monroe" dresses. Her uncle shot himself in the bathroom after they left Cuba. She can always hear it in her head. She still smells like sugar cane.

Hal Ludacer is more beautiful than Greta Garbo.

Patty Astor is Fab 5 Freddie's girlfriend. She wears the highest stiletto heels in town.

Alba Clemente was an avant-garde performance artist in Italy. She is more elegant and exotic than anyone else.

Maripol is a jewelry designer and looks like Coco Chanel. She creates the black rubber ring bracelets that everyone wears.

Z. was a prostitute in Japan.

Edit Deak is older than everyone. She is Hungarian. Everyone hangs out in her loft on Wooster Street. She says she once communicated with a panther in a Hungarian zoo.

Tina Chow has the longest, skinniest arms.

Fab 5 Freddie is a good kisser.

Lady Pink is the only female graffiti artist. She spray paints kittens.

I cannot remember everyone on the scene. Jean always boasted that he had slept with them all. I knew he was lying.

FROM SATURDAY TO MONDAY

Jean-Michel listens to jazz. He listens to Charlie Parker, Miles Davis, Max Roach, Hip Hop, Blues and Latin and African music. One day he finds out that Billie Holiday does not have a gravestone on her grave and he can think of nothing else.

He calls Diego Cortez. Cortez is one of Jean-Michel and Suzanne's first friends. He is an art curator and dealer who knows everything about the club scene and the art world. He is always impeccably dressed with a European air of elegance about him. Jean-Michel and Suzanne adore him. Jean-Michel says he is a 'queen – but you would never know it.'

From Saturday to Monday Jean-Michel and Diego Cortez spend hours designing Billie Holiday's gravestone. Every-day Suzanne is sent out to buy them coke.

'Boom for real!' Jean-Michel says when they finish.

Jean-Michel says his paintings are jazz on canvas. He makes his own music also.

One day he buys himself a TEAC reel to reel recording machine and composes experimental, improvised music and poetry. He makes tape loops that he then records one over the other as if they were musical instruments. He does this a lot with Michael Holeman and Nick Taylor.

At four o'clock Jean-Michel calls the suicide hotline and has a conversation with the man on the other end of the line. Jean-Michel says 'Hijacked Marlboros' and 'You won't be so arrogant once the police arrive' and 'It's gone soft'. The man at the suicide hotline is convinced that Jean-Michel has stolen a truck of Marlboro cigarettes and feels guilty and wants to commit suicide. The man says, 'What's gone soft?' Jean-Michel says, 'You won't be so arrogant once the police arrive'. The man says, 'I'm not being arrogant'. The conversation goes back and forth. Jean-Michel makes a recording of this that he later uses with music.

I loved Diego Cortez. He was very funny. He called me Jean's muse. We were good friends. It was Diego who arranged Jean's first group show called New York/New Wave at a PS1 space in Long Island City. Throughout Jean's career Diego got a lot of important people interested in Jean's work. Without Diego, Jean might never have become famous.

ONLY FOOD

'I love the way you walk, Suzanne. Like you lead with your pelvis with your back slanted and long steps,' Jean-Michel says. He imitates her walking back and forth in the kitchen.

He never buys her presents or clothes. Only food. Whenever he is happy he brings her all kinds of Italian cakes and pastries. She has eaten profiteroles, petites fours, eclairs, Japanese jellies, meringues and marzipan. Sometimes the refrigerator is completely filled with these packages wrapped in paper and string.

I don't know why Jean bought me pastries all the time. It was really very funny. I think he thought it was something that rich people did. When he did not have money and could not afford the pastries, he would buy me bags of white and pink marshmallows.

HOW TO DRAW

Jean-Michel never reads. He picks up books on mythology, history and anatomy, comic books or newspapers. He looks for the words that attack him and puts them on the canvas. He listens for things Suzanne says and writes them on his drawings. He listens to the television.

One day he says, 'Suzanne, I'm almost a famous artist now and I don't know how to draw. Do you think I should be concerned?'

She says, 'Well, just teach yourself and there will be no problem.'

Later that day Jean-Michel comes back with seven 'How to Draw' books – *How to Draw Horses, How to Draw Flowers, How to Draw Landscapes,* etc. This was all tongue-in-cheek. He thought the books were hilarious and did several paintings where he copied the drawings.

Jean always did drugs, he never stopped. Whenever he went to Europe or Japan or any new place you could count on it that in a couple of hours upon arriving he knew where to buy what he wanted. It was like he had a radar for it. Once when he came to Canada to get me, within five minutes he was off on my brother's motorcycle buying drugs.

His other major interest was girls, women. He loved women. He loved sex. He always had a lot of women. The only time he was faithful to me was the first few months that I lived at the Crosby loft. He had many small relationships with many different women. He would become bored quickly though. That's why I always had a problem knowing if I was really special to him. I still sometimes don't know. Other people tell me I was. He once told me that the only women he had ever loved were me and Jennifer Goode.

I accepted it.

His main interest was music, though. He loved Jazz, Max Roach, Charlie Parker, Miles Davis, etc. This is what he listened to at the Crosby loft. When he moved to the Great Jones loft he developed a taste for classical music. (I think from Andy Warhol.) He loved making experimental music. He actually put out a record that he produced and put up the money for it. The record was a rap record that he did with the rappers K Rob and Rammellzee. I think he referred to it as Rammellzee versus K Rob. He did the drawing for the cover which was white on black. I think he pressed one thousand of them. I used to have one but I gave it away thinking I could get another but I never did.

His paintings were inspired by the Jazz musicians and he felt akin to them. A lot of the early Jazz artists, of course, couldn't even walk through the front door of the hotels and clubs they were playing in and had to enter through back doors and kitchens and I think Jean felt this was a metaphor for his place in the white art world: he had entered through the back door. He broke into the white art world in a way that had never been done before by a Black.

HE NEVER EATS PORK

Jean-Michel says it frightens him that one day he might accidentally eat pork. When he goes to restaurants, especially Chinese restaurants, he asks the waiters over and over again if the food has pork in it.

His mother taught him this. Jean said that the pig meat can get right into your heart and make it grow. He said many scientists knew this. He said that they had X-rayed people who eat pork and that they have more arteries and veins and that the heart became like a big complicated knot.

BOMBERO, *1983*

acrylic and oil paintstick on canvas
65 1/3 X 90 1/2 inches (165.9 X 229.9 cm)

She hits him. She hits him on the scar and hard into the place where his spleen would have been. For one second her fist is inside his body.

He painted Bombero *once after a fight when I hit him like a man hits a man. I only did it once. I never did it again.*

He had disappeared for days and someone told me that they'd seen him at the Roxy with a blonde. Someone else told me he was living with two black girls in SoHo. Someone else told me he'd gone to LA. I was furious. I went out and picked up a Puerto Rican hip-hop boy who put his gun under my pillow.

Then Jean came back. I told him to get out and that I was going to call the Fire Department. I would never have told Jean that I was going to call the Police. He would never have forgiven me that. Never! So I said the Fire Department and that made him laugh and laugh so I punched him very hard. I know it must have hurt, but he just hugged me and laughed.

Then of course he painted Bombero *a few weeks later but the painting was not funny and the fireman in the painting scares me.*

SCRATCH OUT AND ERASE

'I scratch out and erase but never so much that they don't know what was there. My version of pentimento.' Jean-Michel tells Suzanne as he copies the writing on a cereal box: Sugar Coated Corn Puffs.

I remember the day that some buyer asked Jean for his C.V. He was furious at first because, of course, he did not have one and he had never studied anywhere and I could tell that he suddenly felt a wall stopping him but this only lasted a second. Then he tore out a piece of paper from a copybook that he liked to draw in and wrote something that was full of spelling errors and scratched out words. It was Jean's version of a C.V.. It began, 'Jean Michel Basquiat, born Dec. 22, 1960 in Brooklyn, New York.' He included all the public schools he'd been to since first grade and stated that he'd dropped out of school in the eleventh grade. He wrote that his first ambition in life was to be a fireman, and that his artistic ambition was to be a cartoonist.

This was all written out in a perfectly organized list and printed to look like a serious document. He added his early themes, which he numbered as: the seascape from Voyage *to* the Bottom of the Sea; *Alfred E. Newman; Alfred Hitchcock; Nixon; wars; weapons; and cars.*

I do believe that he wanted to be a fireman since he always stopped whatever he was doing when a fire-engine passed by. He felt a reverence for firefighters and he liked to draw them with their funny hats. He called these hats, 'helmets'.

To this resume he also added that he had failed at life drawing in ninth grade. He was very proud of this and boasted about it, especially when he started making money.

He asked me if he should add his musical influences to the list.

I said, 'No.'

So, of course he did.

He considered music to be his greatest influence and scribbled West Side Story, The Watusi, Walking Harry *and* Black Orpheus *on the list.*

When he finished, he suddenly asked me, 'Do you think they ever asked Picasso for his curriculum vitae?'

'Of course not,' I answered.

He said that if anyone ever asked him for it again he was going to give the measurements of his hand.

He left the apartment and went out to buy a ruler. When he came back he began to measure his hand and write it all down: Right hand with four fingers and one thumb. Palm measures: 3 and one half inches wide and 3 and one half inches long. Small scar on index finger. He also added the length of his fingers and thumb.

Then he really got into this and started to measure his whole body. When he had finished, he measured my body also. he made me lie down on the floor and wrote down all my measurements. He said, he hated to be the one to tell me, but he had discovered that my left arm was shorter than my right arm.

I've always known that.

THE BURROUGHS READING

William Burroughs is reading at The Ritz. Jean-Michel puts on his paint-covered baggy pants and trench coat. Suzanne dresses up in black. They go down past Houston Street and buy some coke. They sniff it in the taxi on the way to the reading.

'Don't talk to me, Venus,' Jean-Michel says, 'I don't want to hear your voice. I hate your Canadian accent.' In a sing-song voice he imitates her and says, 'Mum, Mum, Mum.'

Suzanne is quiet. The coke is sharp and cold in her nose and mouth.

William Burroughs sits on the stage behind a desk with one bright flood light on him. His voice is deep and scratchy and full of alcohol. Jean-Michel watches him silently, like a predator.

When they get home Jean-Michel tells Suzanne to stand against the wall. She lets him move her as if she were a doll. He pushes her against the wall, places her arms at her side and lifts her head. With his fingers he closes her eyelids.

'Don't talk to me, Venus' he says, 'I don't want to hear your voice.' He places a tin can on her head. He places a jar of paint on her head. He laughs. He tells her to open her hand and spits into her palm.

Jean was the one who told me that William Burroughs mistakenly killed his wife. Well, he did not say it was a mistake. He told me the story as if to insinuate that there was a very thin line between love and murder. He had a glint in his eye like he was trying to scare me. Like it was a cool thing that Burroughs killed his wife.

Later Jean got to know Burroughs well and Ginsberg, but I was not with him then. He read Kerouac all the time.

THE GIRL AGREES
TO GO TO PARIS

She can sleep for two days. She can sleep for five days. Once she was able to sleep for seven days and her body fell beneath her when she tried to walk.

Through her sleep-haze she can hear voices. These are the voices of graffiti artists that have come to take Jean-Michel to a graffiti art show at Fashion Moda (the first graffiti art gallery in the South Bronx). Suzanne can hear the voices of Rammellzee, Toxic, A-1, LA2 and Dondi White spewing off their 'Hip Hop' language. 'Where's your freak, Jean-Michel?' 'Watch it boy, he's a real crimee. You know what time it is. Where's your freak? It's word up. Listen bro, all your homies will be there. You know what time it is. Homie Futura 2000 will be there. What a crimee! Where's your freak? It's word up and you know what time it is.'

Jean-Michel disappears for weeks.

Suzanne's mother calls her from Canada.

'Suzy,' she says. 'I've sold everything. It's taken three weeks and I've had two garage sales. Your father bought everything.'

'I think I might die, Mum,' Suzanne says.

'I know, dear. That's why I want you to go to Paris and check up on your sister.'

Suzanne goes to a loft where Jean-Michel is staying to say goodbye. The loft is a mess and Jean-Michel and a blonde, French model are sitting on the bed doing heroin. He tells Suzanne to get out. He tells her that he doesn't love her anymore. He tells her he never loved her and that she is a white Arab piece of shit.

In Paris, Suzanne's sister has a job taking care of an American man who is diabetic. Suzanne and her sister have to iron his clothes and give him massages, which takes forever because he is so fat. He takes them to La Coupole. He taunts Suzanne with his diabetic needles. He says, 'Makes you want some heroin, doesn't it?'

While I was in Paris Jean kept calling me to come home. I never told him that I was taking care of a sadistic, diabetic man and trying to get my sister out of the situation. Instead, I made it sound like I was having a fabulous time. I told him that I had a French boyfriend who was a musician and who bought me stuff. I told him that the drugs were good. Jean was furious. He'd hang up on me and then call back a few minutes later.

THE GIRL RETURNS
TO NEW YORK

Dressed with a glamorous 'Audrey Hepburn' scarf on her head and large sun glasses, Suzanne arrives at the Pyramid Club straight from the airport, carrying her suitcase. She hopes she can find someone to take her in for the night.

Jean-Michel is there with Shenge. He walks up to Suzanne and says in a fast, desperate kind of way, ' I am very rich now and I have a big loft in SoHo – please come and live with me.'

Shenge and Jean-Michel clean up the loft and place flowers everywhere. The refrigerator is filled with pastries.

Every morning Jean-Michel leaves the loft to go and paint in the basement of Annina Nosei's gallery. He returns every two hours to see Suzanne and bring her some cakes. Then he comes home every evening at six.

Jean-Michel lets Suzanne wash his dreadlocks when he sits in the bathtub. They take a long time to dry – like sponges. Suzanne pats them and squeezes them in a towel for an hour.

In the Crosby Street loft there was a coloured TV and a TV stand on wheels that was either in the living room area or would be dragged into the bedroom area. There was a Haitian Voodoo statue that stood about three feet tall with a little bag around its neck. The statue was crudely carved out of dark wood. Jean bought this statue one day and told me to never open the bag around its neck. I never did. He told me never to touch the statue. I never did.

There were lots of toys around. Jean loved toys. Toy trucks and cars, marionettes from Italy. Strange little hand-made toys. There were drawings and papers strewn everywhere in the painting area which was also the living room area. There were books all over the floor or leaning on the wall. The kitchen table had bowls of fruit and flowers on it. Jean always bought me flowers – those red flat plastic-looking things with the yellow penis coming out of them. Those were his favourite flowers. There were bottles of expensive wine. Everything was always a mess. I cleaned it up everyday. He had oil-stick crayons everywhere, hundreds of them. Many were mashed on the floor.

He always shopped at Whole Food and Dean and Delucca on Prince Street in front of the Annina Nosei Gallery. He bought expensive plates and stainless steel pots and pans and utensils to cook with. The refrigerator was always full. He liked fruit mixtures. He bought a juicer and made carrot and vegetable juices. But then he would go and buy expensive Italian pastries or chocolates. He would only buy expensive food.

In the bedroom on the bed was a pale yellow and gold wool blanket with a floral large diamond design and a child's

Superman polyester comforter. There was a black piece of fabric on the headboard shelf. We always went to sleep with a mirror covered with coke right at our heads on this headboard shelf. There was white powder ground into it all over the place.

Sometimes he would stay out for three days at a time on coke and in the clubs with other women. He would not talk to me but he still wanted me there. He had different people over at night. Sometimes it was fun for me. We would sit around the living room coffee table and do coke for hours.

The smell of his sweat came out of my pores.

THE CROSBY STREET
LOFT MADNESS

She irons the clothes, folds his clothes, places them in the same order on the shelf – the red sweater is folded this way and placed above the red shirt. She places the soap at an angle on the sink and always places the towels in the same order 1-2-3. She irons one shirt five times. She makes the bed three times and irons the sheets. If a sweater fades in the wash she cries. She never speaks and only answers questions or speaks in a panicky monologue :

'My mother was a spy in the war. They took her to see a woman with transparent skin. They could see her heart beating in there and her lungs and blood. They could see her eyeballs turning. This was a military secret. Nobody knows about this. And they would give the woman food – turnips, oranges, bread and watch it all go down into her. This was a military secret. I heard about her when I was five and I thought she must have been very beautiful like a larvae, but very scared. I kept looking at my own stomach and wondering what was in there. I chewed carefully. My mother said she was a kind of Venus or virgin.'

At first Jean-Michel thinks this is funny and puts some of her words in his paintings. Then he tells her to shut up. He paints *self-portrait with Suzanne*. He paints her speaking her chicken-chatter, '*PTFME E a a a R M R M O AAAAAAAA.*'

They do coke six or seven times a day. He tells Suzanne she can only wear one dress. It is a gray shift with white checks. He tells her she can only wear one pair of very large men's shoes. He does another line of coke. Suzanne walks clunk-clunk-clunk, her feet wading in the shoes, around the loft. He tells her she can't wear lipstick anymore. He says she can only buy groceries and detergents. Then he says no, he will buy them. He does another line of coke and paints *Big Shoes*, a portrait of Suzanne in big shoes. He calls her, 'Venus'. He says, 'Hey, Venus, come and kiss me.' He says, 'Venus, go get us some coke.' He writes 'Venus' into his paintings and says Suzanne is only with him for his money.

Jean-Michel sticks black paper over all the windows so that they won't know if it is day or night. 'The day is too light,' he says.

Soon Suzanne stops cleaning and Jean-Michel stays at home all day.

Suzanne finds a place to live under a small table, like a small cat that finds a hiding place. From here she watches Jean-Michel paint, sleep and do drugs. He picks up books, cereal boxes, the newspaper or whatever is around. He finds a word or phrase and paints it on his board or

73

canvas. A few times a day he crawls under the table with Suzanne and gives her a kiss on the forehead. Sometimes he pulls her out, has sex with her, and then puts her back under the table and continues to paint.

Sometimes Suzanne weeps a little and Jean-Michel says, 'Shut up, Venus. I know what it is like to be tied up and fed, with a bowl of rice on the floor, like an animal. I once counted my bruises and I had 32.'

Suzanne moves from under the table into a closet in the bedroom. In here there is a green trench coat, a pair of moccasins, black and pink pumps, a tin frying pan, a supermarket plastic bag full of bills, two large boxes of chalk. Under one moccasin Suzanne finds a small box of birthday candles.

BLACK TAR SOAP

Jean-Michel's favorite soap is Black Tar Soap. He uses it everyday. It makes a gray lather. No one else can use it. It is his joke. Jean-Michel draws it on his paintings.

Everything was symbolic to him. How he dressed, how he spoke, how he thought, who he associated with. Everything had to be prolific or why do it and his attitude was always tongue-in-cheek. Jean was always watching himself from outside of himself and laughing.

When he had a blonde girlfriend from a wasp upper middle class family he dressed like a preppy, like a Kennedy. But he would do just one thing to throw the whole thing off, like keep his hair in crazy dreadlocks – and not the dreadlocks you see on anyone.

He tried to make people notice him, wake them up, by using a symbol out of context. This occurred in his paintings and in his actions. He never took anything as it was. Any idea, any belief, any norm was very quickly examined and used in his art.

A GENEALOGY OF HEROES

Jean-Michel loves boxers and musicians. His heroes are Hendrix, Joplin, Charlie Parker, Billie Holiday and Joe Louis. He loves anyone who died from a drug overdose. He says he loves Suzanne also because she is the first woman he has ever met who is a living, walking, breathing cartoon.

Jean had a pair of red boxing gloves. He said he liked to put his hands in them and just lie on the bed and watch television. He said he could feel thunderbolts in them. Sometimes he would bounce and box around the apartment hitting the refrigerator and the walls.

BROKEN BLOSSOMS
THE YELLOW MAN AND
THE GIRL

On the television screen the girl makes herself smile by pushing up the corners of her mouth with the tips of her fingers.

> When not serving as a punching bag
> to relieve the Battler's feelings, the
> bruised little body may be seen creeping
> around the docks of Limehouse.

Jean-Michel and Suzanne are in bed under Suzanne's Superman blanket. They smoke pot, eat and watch silent movies.

> In every group there is one, weaker than
> the rest – the butt of uncouth wit or
> ill-temper. Poor Lucy is one of these.

Jean-Michel sucks Suzanne's fingers.

> Her dreams, her prattle,
> her bird-like ways,
> her sweet self –
> are all is own.

Jean loved silent movies because they were like cartoons. I think that he felt that even in life we should be walking around with a word-balloon above our heads – you can see this in his art also.

He always kept watch for any black characters but, of course, they only appeared as servants, if at all.

We watched D.W. Griffith's Broken Blossoms *dozens of times and Jean could quote whole sections of it: 'It is a tale of temple bells, sounding at sunset before the image of Buddha; it is a tale of love and lovers; it is a tale of tears.' The quote he loved best was, 'The yellow man holds a great dream to take the glorious message of peace to the barbarous Anglo-Saxons . . .'*

I remember he did a few paintings of the yellow man on some cardboard boxes. For a short time he called himself the 'Yellow man' and he called me 'the Girl' or 'Lucy,' using a funny, formal language.

He would say, 'The Yellow Man is desirous of a kiss from The Girl,' etc. This lasted only a short while.

I think he adored Broken Blossoms *because of all the opium-smoking scenes, and there were many boxing scenes also. The mime and mute aspect of these movies moved him deeply. Sometimes, after a session of watching several silent movies he would be very quiet for hours and just mime to me anything he wanted or wanted to say and the apartment would be filled with a strange, quiet feeling as if we were underwater.*

NOT FOR SALE

Jean-Michel is like the child who tells the fat lady on the bus, 'You're fat.'

His paintings scream *Famous Negro Athletes* and *Origins of Cotton*. The words are childishly scrawled backwards or scratched out and placed with provocative images of kings with black crowns covered in tar and feathers. He says, 'There are only fifty people who buy art. They buy whatever I paint because they are white-washing history . . . just like the "Mammy" salt shakers that disappeared.'

He refuses to sell his paintings and writes, 'NOT FOR SALE' on some of them. He is furious because people are writing about his ghetto childhood and call him a 'graffiti artist' and 'primitive'. 'They don't invent a childhood for white artists,' he says.

He wears Armani suits to paint in and throws them away afterwards. He makes fun of everyone by wearing pseudo-African garb to important art openings.

Jean-Michel paints *Obnoxious Liberals* because he says he is sick of liberal white art collectors. He makes Suzanne cope with the people who come to the loft to buy his paintings. He hides in the bathroom.

Suzanne says, 'Please sit down. Can I get you some coffee?'

Jean-Michel comes out of the bathroom and says, 'I don't think it goes with your couch.'

The buyers are insulted. He pours a box of granola on their heads from the window of the loft as they leave. He says, 'I feel like an art mascot.'

He never sells paintings to people he does not like.

Jean-Michel is full of fears, especially when he is all coked up. He is afraid that he will be a flash in the pan. He is afraid that the KKK is going to kill him because he is getting so famous and he is Black. He installs an elaborate alarm system in the loft. He thinks that the CIA is going to murder him.

One day he comes home to the loft with two delivery boys. He has bought a color T.V., a stereo system, a TEAC recording machine. He sits on the sofa looking sad and crying. 'I didn't know what else to buy,' he says to Suzanne. 'Did you want something?'

When he first starts to get rich he rents limousines to take him everywhere. He drives down to the Bowery and throws 100 dollar bills to the bums. He tells Suzanne, 'I have to do this every day.' He remembers that once he and some friends harassed a street bum and poured a liquor bottle over the bum's head.

I met Shenge Ka Pharoah (whose real name was Selwyn O'Brien) before Jean did when I was working at the Berlin nightclub as a bartender. Shenge worked at Reggae Lounge. Then Shenge was always around. He did everything for Jean. He cleaned, ran errands, bought drugs and was a buffer for Jean from people and situations Jean did not want to deal with. Shenge always loved me and always referred to me as Jean-Michel's woman. He had a charming Barbados accent. I think that Jean was probably closer to Shenge than any other friend he had. In my opinion even closer to him than Andy Warhol. Andy was really only around in the latter part of Jean's life when Jean was famous already. Andy was Jean's connection to other famous people.

Jean trusted Shenge with all his secrets.

Shenge was very small, thin, fragile and gentle looking. He had a beautiful face with small features and sparkling eyes. He had a full beard, dreadlocks and soft loose-fitting, flowing clothes and he had a profound spirituality about him. He was always around Jean until the last few months of Jean's life. I asked Jean where Shenge was and Jean told me that they had had a falling out and that they were not friends anymore. This was typical. Every person that was close to Jean eventually had a fight with him. I think it scared Jean to have people get too close.

Shenge was part of the family. I loved Shenge too. Shenge and I still see each other occasionally on the street. We both have this look in our eyes like only the two of us shared some kind of deep experience. We don't have to say anything. We just hug each other and know. Shenge more than anyone knew what I went through with Jean. And I know what he went through too. We are the only people that share both the ecstatic and hellish experience of Jean. Jean behaved a certain way with Andy Warhol. He did not show his whole self to Andy. Because both Shenge and I lived with Jean, we knew the whole person. We knew how deeply compassionate and loving he could be at one moment and then suddenly become cruel, cold and angry. It was basically either me or Shenge who lived with Jean. Most times it was the three of us hanging out.

One night I had been out with Rene Ricard, after living in the Crosby Street loft, and Jean was now living with Shenge at the Great Jones loft. Rene and I were with T. doing coke at a party. Then T. invited us back to his house. Rene told me to go and said he would be back shortly. So I went, but I was really frightened of T. (who is a very famous gallery owner in SoHo). I only went because I thought Rene would be there too. Rene never showed up.

83

Immediately T. began to act very strange. He asked me how big Jean's penis was and if it was true that Jean had herpes. I was very scared.

Then T. took his pants off and started chasing me around with a rolled up newspaper in his hand. I was terrified and I ran out the door. He followed me with no pants on and wearing just a white shirt and a tie. It was really a ridiculous sight. I was very high on coke and scared that he was going to rape me.

In the street I jumped into a cab and went home. I put on my pajamas and tried to sleep but I couldn't. I kept crying and crying. So I put my coat over my pajamas and put on my shoes and sunglasses and I took a bottle of Remy with me in the pocket of my coat.

As I walked to the Great Jones Street loft I drank the Remy to come down from the coke. I was really drunk by the time I got there. I knocked on the door and Shenge answered.

He said, 'You would not want Jean to see you in this state.'

I said, 'Why not? I've seen him in worse states than this. Shenge,' I continued, ' something terrible just happened to me, please I have to talk to him.'

So Shenge let me in. When Jean heard my voice he came running down from the bedroom. He threw the television at *me from the top of the stairs. I was at the foot of the stairs. Shenge jumped in and pushed the television out of the way. Jean ran down and tore off my sunglasses to see my eyes. He was furious that I was drunk and high. He had never been this violent with me before. He hated it that I would get high without him. He somehow felt responsible for this. It was okay if he gave me drugs because he felt that he was there to take care of me.*

'Who were you with?' he yelled.

I crouched down on the floor and held on to his ankles. I was too scared to tell him what had just happened to me.

Jean said, 'I don't want to know what happened. I can't deal with this now. I'm dope sick. Go upstairs and get some sleep.'

I was sobbing and I couldn't get up off the floor where I was crouching. So he carried me upstairs and put me in his bed. He said he was going to go out and get some dope and that he would bring me some so that I could sleep.

While he was gone, Shenge came up and asked me what had happened. When I told him he said, 'Don't tell Jean, he would kill T., he would go crazy. No girl, you did the right thing, girl, um, hum, hum, um, hum.' (Shenge would say un, hum, um, um very fast all the time. It was a habit. It was somehow comforting to hear).

Then he said, 'Don't worry girl' with his beautiful sing-song Barbados accent. 'He's is going to get you something so you can sleep, don't worry we will take care of you. You are where you should be, you are home, hum, um, um, hum.'

Shenge was not gay, but he had this very feminine maternal side to him. He was like our mother or something. He looked after us. He was so gentle.

MOTHER COMES TO VISIT

Jean-Michel doesn't like Suzanne's mother. He met her for the first time when Suzanne ran away to Canada to get away from him and he went there to bring her back. He hates Suzanne's mother's English accent. He said that just the way she speaks shows she is patronizing and a racist.

Jean Michel's friends think Suzanne's mother is marvelous and charming. She meets Fab 5 Freddy and Rammellzee. She says she understands Rammellzee and that what everybody thinks is gibberish in his talk is accurate.

Jean-Michel keeps saying over and over again, 'Stay away from my pile of drawings.' Suzanne's mother becomes so fed up with hearing this that she steals one of the drawings.

Later Jean-Michel pretends that Suzanne's mother is invisible. He paints *Native Carrying Some Guns, Bibles, Amorites on Safari*. He tells Suzanne that these paintings are inspired by her mother's visit.

A few days after Suzanne's mother has left, Jean-Michel

wakes up Suzanne in the middle of the night to show her a painting he has just finished.

'It's called *Self Portrait As A Heel*', he says.

DINING OUT

Jean-Michel likes to take Suzanne to fancy restaurants. One night at one expensive Italian restaurant there is a long table with twenty white businessmen having dinner. Jean-Michel says, 'They are the kind who have their own private jets.'

The business men stare, whisper racist remarks and drunkenly laugh at Jean-Michel. They think he is a pimp because he is black and has dreadlocks and is wearing messy clothes. They think that Suzanne is a prostitute. She is heavily made-up and has her hair teased up in a bee-hive.

Jean-Michel tells the maitre d' that he is going to pay for the businessmen's dinner. It costs him $3,000. This is how Jean-Michel laughs back. He does this to fuck with them. Most of Jean-Michel's outlandish behavior has to do with a desire to fuck with people's racism.

I was sound asleep in the Crosby loft one night and Jean-Michel was out clubbing. It was about five in the morning when I woke up because I heard people talking in the living room. There was Jean sitting on the couch with the most gorgeous blonde, young svelte woman. I was livid – how dare he stay out all night and come back with a beautiful woman. I called him into the bedroom.

'Who is that girl?' I asked.

He burst out laughing and said, 'It's not a girl, that's Melody, she's a transvestite, isn't she beautiful? Come out and meet her.'

So I went out and did coke with them.

I later ended up becoming good friends with Melody and her boyfriend of many years, who ran a gallery for a short time. I even showed my paintings in his gallery.

Melody was fabulous, very skinny and so elegant. She had straight thin hair with bangs and wore big black sunglasses. She wore tight little black mini dresses and looked like she was straight out of the 60's. She was a runway model and became famous as the Steven Sprouse girl. She wore light pink frost lipstick and had a thin lipped pout. She was all arms and legs. She looked more like a girl than most girls.

She had not had the sex change yet when I first met her. Then I was hanging out with her one night when she told me that she had recently gone to Switzerland to have the sex change. Her adoptive mother paid for it and bought her the most fabulous Yves St. Laurent dress. We were at some friend's loft. Melody and her boyfriend were staying there and they invited me over to do some heroin.

Melody was prancing around in her new Yves St. Laurent dress and talking about her sex change. She was on hormones and had developed little small round breasts. So I asked her if I could see it, the sex change.

So, like girlfriends, we went in the bedroom and she lifted up her fancy dress and took off her underwear and showed me. It was such a beautiful job. It looked just as real as any girl. She was so happy and proud. Then we started talking. I asked her when she started to feel more like a girl than a boy. She said as far back as she could remember. Melody later married her boyfriend and moved to Iowa. The boyfriend became a shoe salesman.

RAMMELLZEE

He walks or rather glides in big steps leaning backward with a bop in his walk, in a be-bop kind of glide. He wears polyester slacks and silk socks. On his head he wears the hood of a sweatshirt or a hat with ski goggles on it. Sometimes he wears the ski goggles down over his eyes. He talks quickly like Donald Duck and even quacks. Rammellzee calls girls, 'freaks' and boys, 'crimees' for criminals. He wears shiny patent leather shoes. He calls this his 'city look'. In Far Rockaway he dresses in track suits because the cops might harass him. He wears rings on every finger and necklaces. He also wears a long white leather trench coat. There is something hip-hop and 'super-fly' about him. He always carries one or two bottles of Colt 45 beer under his coat.

When he sleeps over at Suzanne and Jean-Michel's loft he never takes off his shoes or hat. He says he does this in case he needs to make a quick getaway.

Rammellzee invented a new language called 'Iconoclast Panzerism'. He says that he was put on Earth to smash the written word apart. He explains that all the letters of the English language come from social change, patriarchal societies, economics and history. He calls himself 'Gangster Prankster'. He explains that his name 'Ramm Ell Zee' means 'ramming the elevation of the way we read from left to right like a Z'. He believes that the written letter in the Western alphabet is a reflection of a culture and philosophy that does not suit him or his brothers.

Rammellzee keeps the finger nail on his pinkie long for sniffing cocaine. He does very geometric paintings shaped like his alphabet and then he makes sculptures of them.

He is a member of the 5% Nation, a radical off-shoot of the Nation of Islam. He says that Jean-Michel has a responsibility to the Black man. He tries to convince Jean-Michel to go to the Black Men's Meetings in Harlem. Jean-Michel tells him that his responsibility to the Black man is fulfilled in his paintings.

Jean took Rammellzee on his first airplane. He was terrified as he had never been on a plane before. And when Jean first took him to Barbetta, a fancy restaurant, he was very intimidated and awkward. He didn't know what to order, or what fork to use, etc.

Once Rammellzee noticed that my shoes were worn out so he took me out to buy some. He was all dressed up in his white leather trench coat with his bug ski goggles on and leaning against a two-tone brown and tan – stretch limousine. He opened the door for me. I said, 'Where are we going?'

He said, in his best sinister Donald Duck voice, 'Wherever you want to go as long as I can buy you a pair of shoes there. That's where we are going my little chickadee ha ha ha ha.'

We ended up at Fayva. Rammellzee didn't know this was a tacky shoe store. It was just a shoe store to him. Then he took me to Tony Roma's Steak House on 6th Avenue for dinner, which he considered a very fancy place. We had wine by the glass and salad and steak and baked potatoes and dessert. It was very lovely. Then we drove around so that I could show off my new shoes. They were simple little black high heels. At the shoe shop counter we had bought red clip-on bows for them. I wore them until they fell apart. They were my Minnie Mouse shoes.

Like almost everyone, Rammellzee had a falling out with Jean. I got the impression that he thought that Jean had sold out to the white art world. But I know that deep down he always loved Jean.

THEY DO NOT KNOW
HOW TO DRIVE A CAR

Shortly after Suzanne moves into the Crosby Street loft Jean-Michel takes her to Italy. He is having a show at the Emilio Mazzoli gallery in Modena. Neither Jean-Michel nor Suzanne know how to drive a car so Jean-Michel pays to bring Kye Eric along to drive them around.

In the airplane Jean-Michel continuously gets up to do some coke in the bathroom. He says he has to finish it up before he goes through customs in Europe. He says he wants to open up the emergency door exit and jump on the clouds.

Suzanne has hepatitis. She cannot lift up her arms.

Jean-Michel sits beside her; he kisses and licks one of her arms.

'Beautiful arms,' he says. 'Venus, I have to paint your arms.'

He takes a blue marker out of his pocket and paints on Suzanne's arm. He paints her humerus, ulna, radius and carpus. He writes, 'animal cell' on the inside of her wrist. He draws a ring around her finger.

'Now you are my wife,' he says.

MODENA, ROME, FLORENCE AND VENICE

Jean-Michel, Suzanne and Kye Eric travel to Italy. They stay in the houses of gallery owners and rich art collectors. Jean-Michel finds drugs wherever he goes. He and Suzanne are very happy.

One day in Venice, Jean-Michel says he has not listened to Charlie Parker in two weeks. He says that if he doesn't listen to Charlie Parker he will go crazy. He says he needs to hear the music or he will not be able to breathe. He says that Italy is just like the United States and everywhere else: there are no Black men in paintings in museums.

'This is why I paint,' he says. 'To get black men into museums.'

They spend all day trying to find a Charlie Parker tape but have no luck. Jean-Michel ends up buying some opera arias sung by Maria Callas. When he gets back to New York he plays the music so loud everyone can hear it outside on the street. People walk past looking up at his windows. He paints, 'AAAAAAAAA' onto his boards and canvases.

THE HOSPITAL
IS VERY WHITE

When the fever begins she thinks it is the coke. When she starts to vomit she thinks it must be the heroin. She cannot stand up. She cannot sit down.

'I feel like there is blood inside of me,' Suzanne says.

Jean-Michel never goes to visit her at the hospital. The doctor says that she has Pelvic Inflammatory Disease. He asks her who she has been sleeping with.

Suzanne says, 'Only my boyfriend.'

The doctor says, 'I'm sorry, but your boyfriend gave this to you.'

He tells her to sleep. He says the I.V. is carrying the antibiotic into her body. He tells her she will feel better in six days. He tells her convalescence will take a month. He tells her she will never be able to have children.

WITCHCRAFT, IT WORKS

Jean-Michel tells Suzanne his mother has always been a kind of witch and knows everything about Haitian Voodoo. He says that she learned this to protect herself. He says that she taught him how to do it too.

He paints the words 'GOLD' and 'YEN' and paints coins into his paintings and then everyone wants to buy them.

'See,' Jean-Michel says, rolling up eight one hundred dollar bills into his pocket, 'it works.'

I don't know exactly how long I had been living there. Maybe about one year and a half. Things were really bad between us. He was doing so much coke and was extremely paranoid. Once I got really fed up and flushed an ounce down the toilet. Of course I was doing a lot of coke too but I just wanted it all to stop. I wanted us to be happy again like when I first moved in and we were not doing so many drugs.

Things were really bad. We went days without speaking. I secretly started doing heroin because I couldn't deal with coming down off five days of coke. Jean started staying out all night in the clubs. He went to Reggae Lounge a lot because Shenge worked there. I introduced them because I used to bartend at Berlin which was attached to Reggae Lounge. Jean would do drugs all night there, sometimes for days on end and slept with other women. This made me crazy but I tried not to show it.

Anyway, the night we were supposed to go to Rome again for another show he didn't come home all night. When he finally did come home I told him, 'I'm fed up with this. I don't sleep with anyone else. You would kill me if I did.'

Then I said, 'I am not going to Rome with you.'

He flew into a rage and started breaking things. I was drinking tequila. It was only about 10 a.m. I wasn't supposed to be drinking because of the hepatitis. He picked up my glass of tequila and smashed it against the wall.

'You are not supposed to be drinking!' he screamed. Then he started breaking other things in the room.

I said, 'Why are you so mad at me? You won't let me breathe without asking your permission. I'll just step aside and you can have your freedom to do whatever the fuck you want. I'm leaving. I have nothing. No money, nowhere to go, nothing. But I would rather be out on the street than to live like this.'

Jean started packing for Rome. I served myself some more tequila. We did not speak to each other. Jean was shaking *from coming down from a night of cocaine. Then he walked to the elevator to leave.*

He said, 'We promised Rene that he could stay in the apartment while we were gone. Don't leave the loft until I come back.'

Then he handed me one thousand dollars.

'If you need more money you can go to Annina's and get it,' he said.

I said, 'I don't need your money.'

He threw the money on the floor and left.

That night Rene Ricard took me to a party because I was so depressed.

He said, 'Don't worry. Everything will be okay, you've just never stood up to Jean-Michel like that. It is the best thing you could have done.'

While we were at the party Jean arrived. He wanted to know what I was doing at the party.

Apparently he had gone to the airport with Annina and told her, 'I can't go – I have to go back and talk to Suzanne.' Annina was furious and left without him. Jean left the party and took another airplane to Rome. I went back home to the loft.

Late that night, in the middle of the night, Rene started ringing the door bell. I looked out the window and could see that he had brought one of those stick-up kid tricks home. The kid looked like a thief so I ignored them and didn't let them in.

'You bitch! You bitch!' Rene yelled at me from the street.

The next day Rene came over and he was furious.

He said, 'You weren't even supposed to be here. You were supposed to be in Rome with Jean-Michel. That was a gorgeous guy from 10th Street I scored last night. You embarrassed me.'

I said, 'You can't bring your stick-up, banshee boys here.'

I went into the bathroom and lay down on the bathroom tiles. This was all just too much for me.

Rene came in after a while and caressed my hair.

'Please forgive me,' he said.

Rene and I managed to live for about one week together without any major fights. One day the phone rang and it was

Annina in Rome. She did not know where Jean was. She told me to go to her gallery and get some money and come to Rome immediately. I told her that I could not go, that Jean and I were in a big fight.

I hung up the phone and asked Rene, 'Where's Jean?'

He said, 'You really want to know? She's ten times more famous than you and she's a model.'

'Where is he?' I asked.

Rene said, 'They are in Japan and they are in love. And, the reason I am here is because Jean paid me to get you out of here.'

I knew that this was a lie. But it still hurt. So, I left.

SUITCASES
AND OTHER BAGS

She is very quiet. In one suitcase she places her fish-net stockings, polka dot skirt, dresses, shoes and winter coat. In another bag she packs her passport and plastic jewelry. She takes a small bag of coke out of the refrigerator and hides it inside her hair fastening it with hair pins. She leaves the one thousand dollars that Jean-Michel gave her in the loft. She leaves her typewriter, her coat and her hair brush. She knows you must always leave your hairbrush behind – it's voodoo.

Outside she sits on the sidewalk with her bags all around her. Six punk, hip kids walk by and ask her what is wrong and she tells them, 'My boyfriend doesn't love me anymore. He has other girls. He is famous.'

The boys take her to their house in Alphabet City. Suzanne sleeps on the couch and they give her American cheese sandwiches for four days. She gives them the coke that is hidden in her messy hair. They watch her take it out. They say she is a magician.

One day she stands up and says, 'Thank you, boys. I need to get a job.'

*   *   *

She gets three jobs – working at a second-hand clothing store, an after-hours bar and typing scripts for Eric Mitchel, the underground film-maker.

One month later Suzanne goes back to the Crosby Loft to pick up her typewriter. Jean-Michel is back. He is there with David Bowes, Fab 5 Freddy and some other friends. He looks thin and dirty. Suzanne walks past him to get her typewriter. Jean-Michel follows her.

'Are you coming back? Come back. I couldn't find you. Where were you? I told Rene to take care of you and not to let you leave,' Jean-Michel says.

She knows she cannot come back. Inside her arms she feels that she can carry a piano. She can carry a truck. She knows she can walk, that her legs won't fail her. As the elevator door closes she can hear Jean-Michel breaking things.

Maybe it is the day to go buy some heroin . . . The girl takes a cab past Houston Street and buys some dope. She opens the package in the cab, bends over and sniffs it off of her lap. She thinks about the words she loves: rabbit, rain, Rome, Rammellzee, rocket. She giggles to herself when she thinks that dope makes her mind wind up and around alliterations. Her neck and hands feel warm like fur.

A few weeks later she runs into Jean-Michel when she is buying some dope on the Lower East Side. Jean-Michel takes her for a ride in his limousine. They sniff the dope in the car. Jean-Michel says, 'Burroughs was a junkie, Parker was a junkie . . . it is the road to genius.' At a red light he gives one hundred dollars to a skinny black bum.

'Do you want some money, Venus?' he asks Suzanne.

'No. I never have wanted your money, Jean,' she says.

'I know,' he answers.

COMING BACK
FOR GOOD AGAIN AND
AGAIN

Jean-Michel is made for the night, like a mole. The daylight hurts, the sun hurts, but at night he is transformed into a magician, a Merlin with everything wound up tight and sparkling. Nights are for drugs. Drugs are for nights. In daylight he looks for his shadow and crawls up inside it.

Jean-Michel stands at her doorstep. Suzanne says, "No, no, no, you can't come back." He is disheveled. One of the soles of his shoes flaps open and she can see his toes. He is unshaven. He brings no belongings with him. He does not expect her to take him in. Like all stray animals, he knows he will not be taken in.

I always took him in. I'd convince myself that I wouldn't but then he'd appear with the resigned look of someone accustomed to being turned away – a boy without a friend.

When I'd take him back, which was happening all the time, I'd make dinner for him and run out and buy a really good bottle of wine, even if it took away half of my rent money. I loved to spoil him and he always appreciated expensive things, as if consuming them would make him valuable.

I would light a candle and sit him at the table. He would look at the bottle of wine for a long time.

On one of these occasions we sat together quietly and I did not know what to say to him since this had happened so many times now. We felt a bit like strangers and I made some idle chit-chat and asked if his paintings were selling well. He said that he was making tons of money now. Jean drew himself up straight and said, 'I am famous just like I told you I would be.'

We talked for some time of how he had always painted and how, as a child he had dreamed of being a cartoonist. 'The only thing that has ever interested me,' he said, 'is a blank page.'

That time, for the first time, he also talked about his childhood. He told me how he had always been in trouble and had gone to so many different schools. He also told me about the time he had gone to live in Puerto Rico with his father, when he was eight and after his parents were divorced.

I guess he was lost for his mother. His mother had taken him to art museums and used to paint with him in the afternoons with both of them lying on the floor on their stomachs. She used to paste his drawings up around the house. The loss of his mother had left him with a great sadness. Even though she was now close by at the institution she was far away from him in his mind.

The next morning I gave him an apple to take with him as he was leaving. He said goodbye to me and then five minutes later he came back to the apartment and said goodbye to me again.

'You are my best friend,' he said. It was so sad. That is something children say in kindergarten.

THE VENUS XEROXES

Jean-Michel draws Venus and writes 'VENUS' on dozens of pieces of paper. He Xeroxes the papers, tears them up and hands them out to friends and strangers on the street. This is how he symbolically announces his break-up with Suzanne. He also pastes these Venus' on some of his paintings.

One night Suzanne goes out to the Roxy and finds Jean-Michel with Madonna. Suzanne throws herself at Madonna and starts pulling her hair, scratching and punching her.

'You are with my boyfriend!' Suzanne says.

Jean-Michel just laughs and laughs.

Later he tells Suzanne, 'Well, you beat her up just like a Puerto Rican girl.'

Later he paints *A Panel of Experts*. In this painting Suzanne 'Venus' and Madonna are two stick figures having a cat-fight. On the collage he crosses out the word 'Madonna'.

'Why did you do that?' Suzanne asks.

'Because you won, Venus,' Jean-Michel says.

Jean took me to a party at Julian Schnabel's house. Jean got all dressed up but he would not let me get dressed up. Jean made me wear his long-sleeve overalls that had paint all over them. I was embarrassed. All the other women were all dressed up and looking very beautiful.

Jean laughed at Schnabel's work. He thought it was a joke. He envied how Schnabel was, how powerful and rich he was. He had no respect for his work but he did respect how Schnabel could propel himself to such a position in the art world. Jean was very conscious and fascinated with people that understood how to do this. He had great respect for people who could improve their lot in life. I think that this is also what he loved about Madonna. And also why he loved Andy Warhol. Jean greatly respected Warhol because he was so famous and had such an interesting life and because he hung out with so many famous people. But deep down Jean thought he was a much more talented artist than any of them. Jean really believed that he was a great artist.

As for Keith Haring, they were friends. Jean went back and forth with him: friends and not friends. Jean had very mixed feelings about Keith's work. He loved it that Keith gave the graffiti artists an open door. But, at the same time, he felt that Keith's work was a bit contrived. Jean once said to me that it was 'formula art' and that Keith had found a good thing, that he just did it over and over again. Jean resented it,

111

though – that it took a white guy to bring graffiti to SoHo. Keith hung around with black and Puerto Rican graffiti artists and had a lot of them collaborate on his work, especially a guy called LA2. It was Keith that really made the graffiti artists legitimate. I think his influence in this was greater than Jean's.

Jean was very nervous about how he appeared all the time and was always thinking of strategies. If Jean made the wrong move it was much more dangerous than if Keith made the wrong move. Jean was the first black to be seen as a legitimate artist in the white art world. He had to secure his own place before he could help the graffiti artists. This is why he did the Fun Gallery show. This gallery was owned by Patti Astor in the East Village. Jean had already shown his work in SoHo. He did this show to demonstrate his solidarity with the graffiti artists. It was also a very hip show. Jean would only put himself out for others if it also helped his own career.

INSIDE A TELEPHONE BOOTH

Suzanne spends a month living with friends and then moves back into her own apartment that she had sublet for a year. The place is covered with paintings Jean-Michel gave to Suzanne. She thinks it looks like a shrine. Even the refrigerator is covered with his doodles.

She takes everything down. She throws some drawings and paintings out of the window and they fall on the roof below. The next day someone cleans the roof and everything is thrown out.

Suzanne makes up a spell. She places four 'Venus' paintings in a plastic garbage bag. She buys a can of lighter fluid. It is midnight. She walks to Jean-Michel's loft taking three steps at a time and then turning around three times. She does this until she gets there. It takes her an hour and makes her very dizzy.

On the sidewalk in front of Jean-Michel's loft she pours lighter fluid on the paintings and sets them on fire. It makes a small bonfire.

Jean-Michel looks out of the window to the street below and yells, 'Suzanne, what are you doing?'

She hides inside a telephone booth.

Jean-Michel yells out once more, 'Suzanne, I can see you. Niña what are you doing?'

She does not answer. Her heart beats fast like a chicken heart. AAAAAAEEEEEEAAAAEEEE.

L. A.

The spells don't work. The girl sleeps with ten different boys in two weeks and it doesn't work. She kisses a girl at the Pyramid Club and nothing changes.

Suzanne packs her clothes and puts her heroin inside her hair. Jean-Michel sends her a first class ticket to L.A.

On the airplane she sits beside the Country/Western singer Mac Davis. He is wearing a cowboy hat, cowboy boots and a belt of matching lizard skin. It makes Suzanne giggle.

She gets up and goes to the bathroom and sniffs some heroin and puts on some more red lipstick.

If the airplane crashes she does not care.

Jean, Rammellzee and Toxic were at the airport to greet me. We drove in a pickup truck on the freeway to Larry Gagosian's house in Venice. Jean was living in Larry's house. Jean had a studio for painting on the ground floor with a bed in the middle of the room. There was paint and canvases and oilstick everywhere. Jean would go off and leave me alone in Larry's house. Larry had a lot of art and every single door to every room locked automatically behind you when you shut it. They forgot to tell me this and one day I was trapped in a room for hours. In L.A. we used to go to Mr. Chow's where Jean would exchange art for dinner. Jean was friends with Tim Kelly who was the son of Gene Kelly. Once we went over to Gene Kelly's house to see Tim. It was a grand old Hollywood house and there was an Oscar on the mantelpiece. I was leaning over the bar with my ass in the air trying to get a drink and in walks Gene Kelly. I was floored. He was an idol of mine. Tim introduced us and I shook his hand. Gene Kelly apparently loved Jean and gave him his jacket from Singing In the Rain.

Jean told me that Madonna had been there to visit him the week before I came. Madonna, he said, had asked him to take her on a shopping spree. He asked me why I never asked him to do this and I answered that it never occurred to me to ask him for such a thing.

Then I said, 'Will you take me on a shopping spree?'

And he said, 'No. I'm completely broke from Madonna's shopping spree.'

MICHAEL STEWART

It does not take long to find a nice, sweet pair of arms. A kid's arms. A boy who is even more of a child than she is. He is gentle. He has never felt the whack of a hand to the back of his neck. He has never felt a punch to the side of his face. He has never known his skeleton.

Suzanne meets Michael Stewart at the Berlin nightclub where she is a bartender. He is a bus-boy at the Pyramid Club. Michael Stewart is a shy, light-skinned Black man. He comes from a very nice Baptist middle-class family in Brooklyn.

When Suzanne is in the hospital with PID, that she contracted from Jean-Michel, Michael comes to visit everyday. Suzanne is there for two weeks on IV antibiotics and he brings magazines, Coca-Cola and potato chips. They spend New Year's Eve in the hospital together.

I'll never forget how sweet and kind Michael Stewart was. I adored him as if he were my kid brother. He was gentle and quiet. When I was sick in the hospital he came to see me everyday. He'd do all the things I could not do like pay my phone bills, etc. He was a little bit awed that I was Jean's girlfriend.

THE BERLIN

Michael sits at the bar and asks Suzanne for a coke and talks to Suzanne for hours. He comes in every night he can. He chews on toothpicks and eats the olives and cherries out of Suzanne's bar tray.

They play tic-tac-toe and geography games. One night Suzanne leans over and kisses his forehead. She tells him he reminds her of her little brother. He tells her he has nowhere to live and she lets him live with her.

He asks her if he can use the shower and Suzanne says, 'Sure'.

He asks her if he can drink some of the milk and Suzanne says, 'Sure'.

He asks her if he should go out and buy the newspaper and Suzanne says, 'Sure'.

He cleans the apartment while Suzanne is at work.

They sleep together and sometimes they make love. In the morning Suzanne says, 'You remind me of my brother.'

Once in a while Suzanne disappears for days. She is still seeing Jean-Michel. This never stops.

A few weeks later Michael loses his job and moves back to his mother's house on Clinton Avenue.

LUCKY STRIKE

Suzanne sees Michael at a club on 9th street called Lucky Strike, where Madonna is a bartender. They have a few drinks. Suzanne tells him that she is sorry that she is always going back to Jean-Michel, but that she can't help it. Michael is very sweet and gentle and just strokes her arm and says, 'Yes, yes.'

Suzanne says, 'You can come back and stay with me if you like.'

Michael says, 'Yes, yes.'

After a few hours he leaves the bar and takes the LL subway to Brooklyn.

It is alleged by the police that Michael was writing graffiti, yet no graffiti or markers are found. Michael is arrested. The officer claims that Michael resisted arrest. The arresting officer calls for a backup unit. Five cops arrive.

Suzanne thinks: he was so slight and gentle, I could have put a pair of handcuffs on Michael.

It was about ten in the morning when I got a call from Michael's mother. She told me that some police had come to her home and told her that Michael was in the hospital. She was calling from the hospital. She was in the emergency room. She told me to come. I arrived at the emergency room of Bellevue Hospital and found Michael's parents there. I asked what had happened. They said that they did not know.

Michael's mother was a pleasant, short woman with light skin and a deep sadness and worry in her black eyes that always looked watery like pools. She had a very pretty face with a big thin stretched smile. When she smiled her whole face lit up except her eyes, which always remained sad – probably because of the death of her first son. Michael's father was perhaps the most elegant man I have ever met. A tall thin light-skinned Black man with white features. He always wore a suit and tie and a 40's style hat, which he removed whenever he entered a room. He was quiet, shy and modest like Michael. I was impressed by his dignity. He always sat in the visitor's room reading the New York Times *from cover to cover. He was in terrible pain, you could see it on his face. But he was so silent with it. He just kept reading and reading and reading.*

I asked Michael's mother why no one had told her what had happened and she said all she knew was that he had been arrested and was now in a coma.

I went up to the emergency room desk and said I was Michael Stewart's fiancée (which I wasn't) and I demanded to see him and to know what had happened. I was told that the information I wanted was not available at the time.

I was then approached by a plain clothes detective who immediately started to question me. He asked me questions about Michael. Did he do drugs? I said, no. Was he known to be violent? I said, absolutely not. Then I became very angry and I started to question the detective. The detective said he did not know anything. This I instantly found curious. He was a police officer. It was either one or the other. The police either found him this way or they did this to him. That would be in a police report and the detective would have access to that information. I knew that something was not right. I then asked him exactly what state Michael was in and if he was going to die. The detective whispered, 'Yes.' I told the detective that I would not answer any more questions until I had a lawyer present. I walked up to Michael's mother and I asked her if she knew a civil rights attorney. She said she did.

When the attorneys arrived everything began to move quickly. We were whisked into a private room. Finally, the lawyers and their own doctor were allowed to see Michael. When the doctor came back, he sat down and said, 'There are so many things wrong with your son you should hope that he dies.' We all let out gasps. But no one cried. The doctor told us he was brain dead. He said that he had a massive hemorrhage at the base of his brain that appeared to have been caused by strangulation from an *illegal choke hold with a billy club. He also said that Michael had numerous abrasions and contusions all over his body and lacerations on his wrists and ankles that appeared to be from handcuffs and foot shackles.*

THE NEXT MORNING

Suzanne calls Fiorucci's where she is working for Maripol, the jewelry designer. She says that she will not be coming to work. Suzanne cuts her hair. She goes to a thrift shop and buys a conservative pink blouse, a black skirt and a plastic string of pearls. She calls Jean-Michel's loft but no one answers.

She borrows a friend's camera and goes to Bellevue Hospital. Michael is in a room with a police guard outside the door and a video camera in the room. They tell Suzanne this is because Michael Stewart is under arrest. She tells the police officer, 'Sir, mister, he is my boyfriend. Sir, mister, please let me in for two minutes. Please, sir, please, mister.'

The room smells of rotten meat. Suzanne throws the coat over the camera and pulls back Michael's sheets and photographs every single mark on his body. His face is covered in small cuts and bits of glass are visible in his flesh. (Later she learns that the police broke the window of the police car with his face). His face is huge and swollen. His eyes are bloated, closed pieces of red and black meat. He has cuts and bruises all over his chest and legs. His head is wrapped in a gauze bandage. Tubes are coming out of his nose and there is a respirator tube in his mouth. There are welts on his ankles and wrists. There is no place on his body that has not been hurt.

She can't touch him. He cannot stand for anything else to touch him. Michael Stewart's parents surrender to this frail, skinny girl who is so strong she can set the world on fire.

I immediately started working with the lawyers on the case. They told me that the most important thing we needed was press coverage. No reporter would cover the story at the beginning. The lawyers told me to go to Peter Noel at the Amsterdam News. So I did. He was the only reporter who would talk to me. I also started meeting with members of the National Black United Front. At first they did not accept me until I told them that I was half-Palestinian.

I also became aware that the lawyers were going to cost a lot of money. As almost every single art gallery in SoHo was showing graffiti art at the time, I went to them and told them about the case. I said that Michael was a graffiti artist. (He wasn't, he just dabbled in it because it was hip). I told them they should donate money for his legal defense. In one month I raised fourteen thousand dollars. The bulk of this money was donated by Keith Haring. Many galleries also donated money and Madonna did a benefit at Danceteria.

After two weeks, Michael died. He died on September 15, 1983. I remember this date so well because I read somewhere that on September 15, 1963 five young girls were killed by a bomb in a church in Birmingham, Alabama by the KKK. I found it a very strange thing that Michael died exactly 20 years to the day of this incident.

The Stewart's lawyers' forensic pathologist found the final cause of death to be strangulation caused by an illegal choke hold with a billy club and a massive brain hemorrhage. The medical examiner for the city, made a formal statement to the press saying that there was no evidence that the injuries sustained while in police custody had caused Michael Stewart's death. When asked by the press what caused the death of a healthy twenty-five year old, he answered, 'heart failure'. It was simply unbelievable.

The lawyers later discovered that someone had Michael's eyes removed. This was not a standard procedure and he should have secured permission from the lawyers and the family. It appeared that someone had also secretly placed Michael's eyes in a bleaching formula that would bleach out the hemorrhaging that could have been proof of strangulation.

A group of us got together and demanded an inquiry into the autopsy report to prove that there was a city cover-up of racially motivated police brutality. We got about four thousand signatures.

I then went with Reverend Daughtery, who was the head of the National Black United Front, to City Hall. We had notified the press and they were all there. Every New York news station and newspaper. Suddenly all the news cameras flashed and Rev. Daughtery said to me, 'Suzanne, I am not in good standing with the mayor, you do it.' I was shocked. I thought that he was going to do it. I instantly became composed and walked up the steps of City Hall by myself and handed the petition to Mayor Koch' s lawyer and said, 'On behalf of the citizens of New York, I present you with this petition that demands a formal inquiry into the Chief Medical Examiner's report concerning the death of Michael Stewart while in police custody.'

A grand jury investigation did ensue, but all the police were let off free. Then a civil suit was conducted and the family received one million dollars for wrongful death. But those police officers are still out there walking the beat.

INVITED TO HARLEM

Suzanne is invited to Harlem to a place called 'Fight Back' to speak about the Michael Stewart case. It is a small room with wall dividers and the walls do not go up to the ceiling. Everyone is Black except for one pregnant Puerto Rican woman and her husband. Suzanne realizes she is in the wrong place. This is a very radical black Muslim 5% Nation meeting. These people believe you should arm yourself against whites. They believe all whites are the devil and they believe in the revolution that will come when blacks will take over the world. They are all radical extremists and followers of Farakkahn.

They ask Suzanne to go up to the front of the room and speak about the Michael Stewart case. Which she does.

A man in the back of the room starts screaming, 'White bitch, white girl!' He is asked to leave the room.

Five minutes later this man returns with a ski mask on his face and a gun, which he points at the door. 'White bitch, you're dead,' he screams. Someone jumps up and shuts the door on this man.

Suzanne cannot swallow. Her mouth moves and says, 'I am a follower of Islam. If I must die I will die in the name of the almighty Allah.'

Everyone stands up. Everyone is suddenly very frightened. The women crowd around the pregnant woman and the men crowd around all the women and they leave together in a huddled mass.

After this, Suzanne stops working on the Michael Stewart case. She is frightened and moves back to Canada for a few months, afraid that she might be deported. She thinks her telephone is bugged and that people are following her.

MICHAEL STEWART'S FUNERAL

Michael's mother has chosen to have an open casket. Even though the body is very badly beaten and even though an autopsy was performed. She wants everyone to see what was done to her son. She speaks at the funeral. She says something short and simple. She says something like, 'When Michael was a little boy, I taught him to believe in justice. I taught him that if he treated people the right way he would be treated the right way. The first song he learned to sing was "God Bless America".

The designer Dianne Brill donates a suit for the burial. Dozens of news cameras are waiting outside the church.

The girl is wearing a tight black skirt and black fish-net stockings.

Suzanne says, 'Michael would have liked me this way.'

The girl puts three of her bracelets in the coffin.

I don't believe in god. But I do believe that each of us has some sort of inner dynamic, that we are not always aware of, that guides us in life to witness certain profound things.

These profound things change us forever and bring us closer to our ultimate selves. My relationship with Jean-Michel Basquiat and the death of Michael Stewart were experiences of this nature.

UNTITLED,
(DEFACEMENT)

Jean-Michel paints *Untitled, (Defacement)*, 1983. Acrylic and ink on wallboard, 25 x 30 1/2 inches. The painting is of two policemen beating up a small, child-like black figure that already appears to be in a shroud. The head is surrounded by a halo. There is graffiti in the background. It says: C.O.P., hoh and DEFACIMENTO?

Jean was very upset by Michael's death. It made him feel very vulnerable. But, at the same time, he was very mad at me for causing such a fuss over Michael's death. He even told me that I should forget about it, that it was over and done with, and that there was nothing that I could do about it. He hated that I was working on the case and that I was so obsessed with it. I think it really frightened him. I think he thought he was next. He always thought that the police, the government, or the people in charge were going to kill him. He was such a barometer for the racist culture he lived in. He felt everything around him in a very heightened way. It was not only cocaine paranoia.

BAREFOOT

Jean-Michel calls Suzanne and tells her to come over. He actually says, 'Come over and play, Venus.'

He is free-basing coke because he has developed a hole in his nose and has a piece of cotton stuck in one of his nostrils. He is wearing a blue Armani suit that is covered with paint. Jean-Michel is so skinny the suit flaps around his skeletal body. He is barefoot and there is paint all over his flat, wide feet. Suzanne does some coke too.

Jean-Michel tells Suzanne to lie down on a canvas that is on the floor. She lies down feeling the pitter-patter of the coke inside her. Jean-Michel draws a line around her body, over her head, down her arms and in and around of her fingers. He tells her she can get up. They do some more coke.

Then he fills in the life-sized portrait with a liver, heart and spleen. He draws two eggs for eyes and a big water-melon mouth. He kisses the face in the drawing but he does not kiss Suzanne.

When they start to come down from the coke they go to bed and shiver and shake in each other's arms.

I first met Keith Haring at Club 57, which was in a basement of a church on 8th Street. He was a really nice guy. Jean introduced him to me. He and Jean had a great deal of respect for each other. But my strongest association with Keith was at the Club Paradise Garage. This was a huge loft club with no liquor license. It was mostly a Black and Puerto Rican club. It was so cool. There was no liquor so everyone came high on mushrooms, pot and mostly hallucinogens like ecstasy and acid. Jean went there a lot and so did I. But usually not with each other. He would see me there and get mad. He didn't like me hanging out there because this club was a really tough Black club. There were metal detectors at the door and there were not that many girls that hung out there. I guess Jean thought he would have to keep an eye on me.

I used to go with Andre Walker who was an underground black gay fashion designer and Leslie Macayza. Leslie and I were the 'Andre Walker girls' because we used to model for him. Jean used to come to these fashion shows and not speak to me but just stare.

Anyway, Paradise Garage had terrific music and Keith Haring was always there and threw parties there too after his openings.

I actually became better friends with Juan Dubose who was Keith's lover. Juan and I were like the girlfriends of the famous artists. We related to each other in this way. Juan was a DJ and we started working on music together. I would

134

go to the loft where he lived with Keith and put on a music track and I would sing over it. Juan collected records and they were hung all over the walls.

I went to visit Juan in the hospital when he was in the beginning stages of AIDS. There was a red sign on the door that said 'Restricted Area, do not enter without a mask from the nurse's station'. I had to wear this paper mask over my nose and mouth. I went in the room and sat down. I brought Juan a box of all my favorite things. My Black Hollywood book (about famous Black actors), some crystal buttons to sew on a shirt and my Michael Jackson Thriller picture disk. This was one of the only ones he didn't have. We didn't mention AIDS. After this, I saw him once more when we got high on dope together in my apartment. He died a few months later.

In the last years of Keith's life he was quite open about having AIDS and he was very active in the Gay Men's Health Crisis and ACT UP. I would see him driving his car around the East Village. He was pale and thin. This made me very sad. And then Keith died. A big memorial service was held for him but somehow I didn't know about it and I didn't go. This made me cry.

Keith was an amazing person. It was really he who brought graffiti into the SoHo galleries. He opened the door for it and made it legitimate somehow. He was a real social radical. He was always working for the underdog. In many ways he was a civil rights worker. The white art world disgusted him. I think he was a lot more responsible for bringing graffiti into SoHo and the East Village than Jean was. Jean was black and had to present himself as separate from graffiti somehow. Keith was gay and white and could glamorize graffiti in a way that Jean could not. Jean and Keith both understood this.

Jean could only be seen hanging around with Toxic, Rammellzee, Dondi White, A-1, Futura 2000 and other graffiti artists when he had already established himself as a legitimate artist at Annina's. He was always very conscious of how he was perceived. It was a real struggle for him, being Black, to be seen as separate from the graffiti artists. Even though he admired it and it was in his roots and he used it to start his career, he was never deep in the graffiti scene. The graffiti he did under the pseudonym 'Samo' in the late 70's and early 80's had nothing to do with classical graffiti – like the kind that was being shown at Fashion Moda in the Bronx, or on trains. It was quite different.

Keith's function was different than Jean's, but both were pioneers. Jean struggled with this. But the two had great respect for each other. Keith painted A Pile Of Crowns *for Jean-Michel Basquiat after Jean's death. He had a big heart. As he knew me since I was twenty, he always said that he had seen me grow up. Once he gave me a bright red yo-yo that had a music box inside of it so it sounded like bells when it went up and down.*

He always called me, 'Jean-Michel's girl'.

AIDS

Maybe you can get it from tears . . .

First she sees an arm, long and thin stretching out of the apartment next door and a skeleton hand placing the garbage outside.

Maybe you can get it from tears . . .

The first person she knows who dies is Martin Bourgone. He is a good friend of Madonna's and helped to manage her career at the beginning. Madonna buys him a lovely apartment so that he can die with dignity.

A dozen people are sitting around the bar at Pyramid. Everyone is talking about how many people they have slept with.

Most everyone says they have slept with about twenty people.

Suzanne says, 'Well, I, I'd say fifty'.

Martin boasts of at least two hundred.

A month later he dies.

NOTHING SEEMS TO FRIGHTEN HER

Suzanne drinks a cup of coffee. She smokes ten cigarettes, lighting one after the other. She writes, 'She makes hungry where most she satisfies' on the wall above her bed. She mops the floor that is still embedded with paint and paintstick. AIDS test: negative.

She wonders where Sammy is and all those children who came to her house dressed in too many coats and sweaters. Suzanne thinks about how faraway she is from Canada and her father's paint fumes that made her feel sweet. Maybe she was not born there. Maybe none of that ever happened. She touches the scar on her forehead. AIDS test: negative.

She wonders how are people going to live if they cannot touch each other's bodies. She promises: God, if I am negative, I promise I will never do dope again. I will never sleep with strangers again. I will never see Jean again. AIDS test: negative.

Inside the second avenue and ninth street phone booth: 'Yes, dear, let me get your file. It's negative, Miss. Thank you for calling.'

But she does not believe in God. And she breaks all her promises.

EARTH, 1984
ACRYLIC ON CANVAS, 66 X 60 INCHES

Textured yellow paint beneath a big, black circle. Hints of a continent appear: Africa in a lion's mane, Africa in the sun and dry, yellow grass. Africa where there are no shadows and the night extends overhead like God's palm.

Jean never talked about going to Africa but when he met blacks from Africa he was awed by them. He became very silent and his breathing seemed to stop. I thought he felt like a fake. Someone once sent him an African sculpture carved out of wood. He loved it and then he gave it away to someone. He always like to give away things he liked. Once he gave me a silver, Mexican ring with a turquoise stone in it, but I was just like him and I gave the ring away. I also threw away piles of his drawings.

Jean was so strange about giving things. First, he'd give the thing, whatever it was, usually a drawing but later it became Armani suits, and expensive bottles of wine and jars of caviar. Then when you got into a fight with him he'd ask for it back. And you gave it back, of course. Then after an hour, a day, a month or a year he'd accuse you of not liking the present because you gave it back to him. No matter how many times you insisted that it was he who wanted it back he would never admit it. He always would say that you didn't like it. So then you'd say, yes, give it back, I do want it. Then he would look at the ground and shuffle his feet around a bit and say he'd given it to someone else. He did this to everyone.

Later, I remember, he once had a fight with Madonna and she returned a whole pile of drawings that he'd asked for. He was very angry that she had returned them. I said, 'But Jean you asked her to return them.' He said I could have them and I said that I did not want Madonna's drawings. He told me to stop acting like a second-rate Italian drag queen.

THE GREAT JONES LOFT

Even after she has stopped living with him she goes over to the Great Jones loft and stays with him – sometimes for weeks. He paints. They have sex, eat, do heroin and drink the most expensive wine. Suzanne never wants to leave. She never wants to open the door. She always feels sad.

They watch a lot of television. If Jean-Michel hears an interesting word or phrase, he jumps up and paints it on his canvas. Friends, art critics, photographers and dealers come and go and Suzanne hides in the bedroom.

She thinks that Jean-Michel has become like a shaman. He is so thin there are no muscles left in his body. The dope has turned him into a ghost. His eyes are luminous and huge. He says he knows he is going to die from AIDS, so what does anything matter.

Jean's favourite restaurant was Barbetta on 46th street. He took me there many times. Sometimes with Shenge. Once with Rammellzee. Rammellzee was very uncomfortable there. He thought it was too fancy for him. Jean had a 'house account' there and never paid. The manager loved Jean and so did all the waiters. Jean always left enormous tips. The manager always went down to the wine cellar and

142

brought back some one-of-a-kind spectacular red wine for Jean.

Once I was there with Jean and Andy Warhol and other friends. Andy started picking up the spoons off the table and signing them with a big black marker and handing them out to the people at the restaurant. Then Jean started signing the spoons with crowns on them. Then a whole signing frenzy started between the two of them. They began signing anything they could find on the table. One girl was wearing a black leather coat and both Andy and Jean started signing and drawing all over it.

Sometimes we went alone and Jean would order all the most expensive things as well as a private stock wine from the wine cellar. Then before the meal arrived, he would go to the bathroom and do coke and come back and not want to eat any of the food and we would leave.

The strangest times, however, were when it was only Jean, Andy and me. Andy was very much in love with Jean and so he was jealous of me. I was always on guard with Andy. In front of me he would describe how beautiful other women were to Jean. They were usually very famous women or models. Andy would go on and on and say, 'She wants to meet you. She told me so.' Jean would act as if I weren't even there and say, 'Really?' like he couldn't believe it. If I got upset or looked angry, Jean would get furious and we would get into a fight for days. Andy knew this and delighted in it.

I very quickly learned what he was trying to do and sat expressionless or, if I had the energy, I would say, 'Yes, isn't she divine? She is enough to make me want a female lover.' This enraged them both.

It was a constant struggle to be with Jean when he was with Andy. Andy couldn't stand to share Jean in any way and Jean loved to feel that he was so important. Jean loved Andy because of this adoration and he loved to feel the power he had over Andy.

Andy was always taunting me. He would say things like, 'Jean-Michel and I have discussed whether or not you are a lesbian. Are you? You would make such a glamorous lesbian. It could make you very famous.' Or he would say things like, 'What would you do if Jean-Michel left you? Would you commit suicide? I don't think his paintings would be so good if you committed suicide.'

I would answer, 'Do you think I am so naive? He has already left me.' And Andy would respond, 'Oh, are you referring to his infidelities, they mean nothing to him, he will always do that. You must be used to that by now.'

On some level I think Andy was talking to himself, trying to console himself.

THE PAINTER
LIKES TO SHOP

One day Jean-Michel, Suzanne and Andy Warhol go to Balducci's to buy caviar for a party. Jean-Michel looks like a bum. His dreadlocks are matted against one side of his face and his clothes are wrinkled and look as if he has not changed them for weeks.

Jean-Michel asks for two thousand dollars worth of caviar. The man behind the counter begrudgingly hands it to Jean. The security guard follows Jean-Michel to the register. He stands close behind Jean ready to arrest him. Jean-Michel never carries a wallet and he begins to take out crumpled ten and twenty dollar bills from his pockets. The customers behind him watch in silence. It is quite a spectacle and takes a lot of time.

When Jean-Michel, Suzanne and Andy leave the store Jean-Michel says, 'boy, did we fuck them!' and bursts out laughing.

Once he started making money he hired limousines to take him everywhere. One day we drove past a garage with an old 1940's Chevy for sale. I said you have to buy that car. He said no. But a month later he bought the car pretending it was his idea. But he never learned how to drive so he hired people to drive for him. When he went to L.A. he shipped the car there along with a driver.

DOS CABEZAS ACRYLIC AND OIL PAINTSTICK ON CANVAS

Jean-Michel paints Andy Warhol's face beside his own face: black and white.

Suzanne asks, 'Why, why does he need you?'

'I recharge his batteries,' Jean-Michel answers.

Jean's drug use worried Andy. Once he called and I answered the telephone. Andy said that he did not want to talk to Jean if Jean was 'out of it'. I know he sometimes told Jean to quit doing drugs but Andy could also be very cynical and would say to him that he'd end up being a legend. Of course Jean loved that! They used to talk a lot about being famous as if that was all that mattered.

THE GIRL
HAS A NEW FRIEND

They are sitting on a stool at a dark and dirty bar on Second Avenue. Suzanne is high on dope. She is dressed in black. She is with her friend Jennifer Clement. Suzanne gets up to go to the bathroom and doesn't come back. The ice in her Remy melts. After forty-five minutes Suzanne returns. She is sweaty and tired.

'What happened to you?' Jennifer asks. 'I was just going to go and get you . . .'

'The bathroom was so dirty,' Suzanne says. 'I couldn't stand it. I just had to clean it. I am just like my mother!'

I met Jennifer when I was waitressing at a Mexican restaurant. She spoke Spanish because she had been raised in Mexico. She had very blonde hair and was a poet. We had a very strong connection the minute we met. We would spend hours after work talking and drinking Remys at a bar. We talked about dark, intense, hungry things. We filled each other up. She comforted me. We held hands at night and walked the streets. We loved each other. We laughed like hyenas. She understood my love for Jean. She wrote poems about it. My love for Jean made her love me more.

When Jean met her he freaked out that a white girl could speak Spanish so well. He did not like it. It disconcerted him. Jennifer was always talking to him in Spanish on purpose because it made him angry. But he liked to show her off to his Puerto Rican friends. He actually liked it that I had a good friend, though.

THE PAINTER
FORGETS TO PAINT

Suzanne bumps into Shenge at the Pyramid club. He tells her that Jean-Michel has been on dope for five days non-stop. He says, 'maybe you should go an see him girl, hum, um, um.'

Suzanne leaves the club and goes to the Great Jones loft. It is two in the morning. She rings and rings the doorbell and finally Jean-Michel answers.

'Oh, thank God it is you, Suzanne,' he says.

Jean-Michel is wearing olive green silk pajamas. He looks a mess.

'Let me give you a bath, Jean,' Suzanne says.

Suzanne washes his body, washes his hair, shaves his face and coos over him as if he were a small child.

Jean-Michel laughs and says, 'Imagine, Venus, my best friend is the whitest guy I could find. He is a fucking albino. What do you think of that? What do you think that means?'

'Andy loves you and he is a genius,' Suzanne says.

'I know you're wondering if I have had sex with Andy. Well, I'm not going to tell you.'

Jean-Michel is dope-sick. He is shaking and feeling nauseous. Suzanne pats him dry.

'I don't care who you sleep with, Jean,' Suzanne sighs.

Jean-Michel tells her to go and get some dope out of the refrigerator. They snort some heroin and go to bed. Jean-Michel sucks Suzanne's fingers. He tells her they taste like rum.

I wanted to make Jean jealous. He was very competitive with other artists like Julian Schnabel, Francesco Clemente, Sandro Chia and Enzo Cucci. He was friends with all of them but very competitive.

I saw Francesco Clemente in a nightclub one night. We didn't really know each other. I was very bold. I went right up to him and said, 'I want you to paint my portrait. I have no money to pay you, but I will pose for you. And I'll do it with my clothes on.' He looked me up and down and said, 'Okay, be at my studio at eleven on Monday morning.'

I went to his studio and we worked together all day for about two weeks. He painted about five large paintings of me. Some were very surreal. He wanted me to stand in the same position for hours at a time while the sun moved across the windows of his loft on Broadway. He would paint all the colours of the sun changing at different positions in the sky as it was reflected through the windows. My body became very stiff from standing still for so long in one position but he insisted and said it was my idea so I must do it.

At that time he only had the two little girls with his wife Alba. They were very young. The little one was about two or three. They used to run in and out of the studio while he was painting but were always called away by the maid or by Alba. We would always break for lunch and have a large bowl of pasta.

While Francesco painted he would tell me about India, where he spent half of the year. He told me what it looked like and smelled like and how beautiful it was. He loved India. This is how he entertained me, by talking about India. Soon all these stories ran out and I became bored. So I told him he must pay me for posing for him. He said, 'How much would you like? How much do you make as a waitress in one day?' I told him on a good day I made one hundred dollars. So this is what he gave me. And Alba gave me a beautiful pair of leather gloves with fur inside. It was winter time and I had no money to buy gloves. I liked Alba very much. She was one of the most beautiful and elegant women I had ever known.

Anyway at the time that Francesco did these paintings of me a show was being arranged at the Bruno Bishoffberger gallery of collaborations among Jean, Francesco and Andy. A few paintings of me were used in this collaboration. I later found out while having dinner with Andy and Jean that Jean was very jealous and did not know what to paint on the one painting of me by Francesco. So Andy told him to paint fire, which he did. Then Andy said to Jean, 'Should we tell her?' Jean became very serious and said, 'No, don't tell her.' I said, 'Tell me, tell me.'

Then Andy said, 'When Francesco was in India and the other paintings of you were locked up in his loft one of them caught fire and they all burned up. Nothing else in the loft was harmed and no one knows how it happened since there was nothing around that could have started the fire.'

The fire happened the same day that Jean painted fire on the collaboration painting at Andy's Factory. Jean was furious that Andy told me. Then Andy said that they named this collaborative painting – the one Jean painted fire on – Premonition.

Jean yelled, 'Why did you tell her! Now she will know she is cursed and it is better not to know.'

That night I went home with Jean. I was asleep while he was painting and drawing. He woke me up and seemed very anxious.

'Who is a better painter, me or Francesco?' he asked.

I said, 'Leave me alone. I don't want to answer that question.'

But Jean was very persistent. I was secretly happy that he was jealous. So I answered, not really believing it at all, 'Of course Francesco is a better painter.'

He was not angry. He became very curious. 'Why?' he asked. 'Why is Francesco a better painter?'

And I said, 'Because you paint about objects and people in the world, he paints about spirituality.'

Then Jean said nothing else and I went back to sleep.

Later he woke me up again. He was very anxious and presented me with a drawing he had just done and asked, 'Is this spiritual enough for you?'

It was a drawing of me sleeping with a snake floating above my head. Now he was laughing.

BOXING

Jean-Michel is always talking about having a boxing match with Julian Schnabel. He wants to sell tickets to the match. He wants to invite everyone and put posters all over New York. He wants people to place bets. He says he is going to wear an African loin cloth instead of shorts and that throwing paint at each other is allowed.

This never happens.

When Jean-Michel and Andy Warhol do a collaboration at the Tony Schafrazi gallery they make a poster announcing the show. The poster is of Jean-Michel and Andy Warhol dressed in boxing trunks and having a boxing match.

Jean-Michel loves to see artists as athletes. He thinks it is a wonderful joke. On some of his paintings he writes: FAMOUS NEGRO ATHLETES.

WHAT TO DO
IF YOU NEED MONEY

When Suzanne needs money she calls up Jennifer and they go to the Great Jones loft. They stand outside on the sidewalk waiting for Shenge. Shenge opens the door.

'Hello, girls,' he says. 'Do you need some money? Come back later when Jean leaves.'

The girls walk around SoHo. Sit on a park bench and wait. A few hours later they return. Shenge opens the door. He takes one hundred dollar bills out of Jean-Michel's shoes, from under the sofa and from inside the stove. The loft is full of hidden money.

'There, girls,' Shenge says. 'Go pay your rent, hum, um, um.'

THE MARY BOONE
ART OPENING

Suzanne picks up Jennifer in a taxi. Suzanne is wearing an enormous black hat – as big as an umbrella – and black gloves.

'Oh dear, oh dear,' Suzanne says pulling at her gloves. 'I am so scared. I haven't seen Jean for two months. He'll be furious that I came. Oh dear, oh dear, oh dear. Let's go.'

The gallery is packed with at least two hundred people. The crowd spills over into the street. Limousines are lined up for blocks and blocks. Jean-Michel sees Suzanne immediately. Her hat can poke people. She won't take it off.

He takes Suzanne and Jennifer to the back of the gallery. He says, 'You two have to stay here and don't come out.'

At the back of the gallery is a little corner that is separated from everyone else by a rope. Jean-Michel's mother is sitting there staring straight ahead of her with her hands folded neatly in her lap. Every few seconds she opens her mouth wide like a fish and closes it. Suzanne and Jennifer sit beside her and greet her but she does not answer but only nods and nods. The three women sit side by side very properly and quietly watching the opening from behind the rope. They could be on a train, at the movies, or at church.

Everybody in the art scene was there. I had gone with Jennifer and Jean made us sit in a corner in a roped off area with his mother. We sat there in a row on three little chairs and occasionally waved at someone we knew. I actually did not mind this because I was so astounded to meet his mother and see her for the first time. I tried to greet her and speak to her but she was so obviously drugged up and could not communicate at all. I wanted to tell her that I loved her son and that I knew everything that she had done to make him a great painter. I wanted to tell her that I knew he loved her. But I could not say anything to her at all. So, at one point, I just reached over and held her hand and she let me.

THE GIRL CAN ALSO PAINT

The girl goes to Pearl. She buys oil paint, acrylic paint and paint stick. 'I can do this too'. She buys canvas and staples. 'I can do this too'. On the way home she buys a bag of dope. She puts the bag deep inside her hair.

Suzanne staples the canvas to the walls of her apartment. She paints portraits of Jean, Joan Burroughs with an apple on her head and famous white people in black face.

She walks around the East Village with paint all over her clothes. When she waits on tables she has paint all over her hands. She tells the customers at the restaurant. 'My hands are clean. This is only paint. I am a painter.' She pulls up her sleeves and shows them how the paint reaches up to her elbows.

Her house smells of paint. It smells like her father, like her home. It smells like Jean-Michel. She breathes and the fumes that come out of her turn her cigarette smoke red.

My paintings represented a creative catharsis of my relation-ship with Jean. I painted white famous people in black face with red lips, like George Washington on a dollar bill or the American Express man. I painted Malcolm X and boxers. I went to my opening at the Vox Populi Gallery on 6th street in a limousine and an outfit by Andre Walker. He made me a red, white, blue and black dress. A lot of the paintings were in these colours and in gold. I looked like the paintings. I also was wearing a big black velvet turban and black elbow length gloves. It was really a performance piece. I painted Jean on the cover of the New York Times Magazine in white face. Five collectors fought over it. After the opening it sold for three thousand five hundred dollars.

I had a big party afterwards at Mike's American Bar and Grill. Everyone came except Jean. My opening was on a Saturday night. Maripol came to the dinner and she brought the New York Times Magazine with Jean on the cover that came out that same night. This enraged me for some reason. So I left the party in my limousine to look for Jean. I found him at Area but he would not go back to the party with me. So I went back alone.

Jean and Andy went to see my art show the next day. I heard that they were both very quiet while they looked at everything. They did not make fun of me or laugh at my work, which was strange.

Later Jean said to me, 'You are no fool, Venus.' He said he liked the portraits I had done of him because they laughed at him.

After this I could never paint again. I sold all the paintings except the one of Joan Burroughs, which I gave to Jennifer, and I kept three of Jean's portraits because he said he wanted them. He told me he would buy them but I said that I would give them to him, of course. But, somehow, I never got them to him.

A LIST OF GOOD DEEDS

1. When Jennifer visits Suzanne one Sunday afternoon she finds a bag lady sitting in Suzanne's kitchen. The woman is dressed in rags and is covered with scratches, bruises and sores. The woman smells like excrement and sulphur.

'Poor dear,' Suzanne says. She is boiling two huge pots of water. She places the bag lady's oozing, bloody feet inside the pots.

Suzanne says, 'There, there. It might hurt at first.'

The bag lady cries, 'Oooooohme!'

Suzanne scrubs the woman's feet with soap and then swabs them with alcohol.

'We need some fresh socks,' Suzanne says. She tells Jennifer to take off her socks and give them to the lady.

Jennifer takes off her socks. Suzanne carefully puts them on the bag lady as if the woman were a small child.

'There, there,' Suzanne says. 'These will keep you warm.'

*　　*　　*

The bag lady says, 'Ooooooooh me!'

2. Suzanne goes to Houston Street to buy some heroin. Outside the crack and heroin house two of the drug dealer's small girls are playing jump rope with an old, frayed piece of rope.

Suzanne says to them, 'My God little ladies, my God!'

She takes a taxi to F.A.O. Shwartz and buys a bright, rainbow-coloured jump rope. She takes another taxi back to Houston Street and gives the girls the new jump rope.

3. Suzanne is walking down 1st. Street toward her apartment. Two Puerto Rican boys are beating up on another very young Black or Puerto Rican boy. Suzanne says, 'Hey, boys, stop it.'

The boys tell her to mind her own business.

'If you stop it I'll give you each a kiss,' she answers.

The boys pause, laugh and say O.K.

Suzanne gives each of them a kiss.

4. It is 4 a.m. It is Winter. Suzanne is walking home from waitressing a late night shift. Her tips are dis-

tributed in her hair, socks and inside the pockets of her jeans.

She sees an old man asleep in a doorway. She can see that he is shivering and trembling from the cold. She takes off her winter coat, covers the man with it and runs all the way home in only her light-weight dress.

For two weeks she goes to work wrapped in a red and blue flannel blanket.

5. One day Suzanne goes to the Great Jones loft. Shenge is not there and Jean-Michel opens the door.

He says, 'Shit! I have thirty thousand dollar checks, forty thousand dollar checks, ten thousand dollar checks. Checks and checks and Shenge isn't here to go to the bank!'

Suzanne says, 'I'll go to the bank, Jean.'

She goes to the bank and cashes some of the checks. She puts the money into her blouse.

When she gets back to the loft she gives Jean all the money. He takes some and tells Suzanne to put the rest inside the oven.

Valda was a very tall, Latvian American. She wore her hair very short like a boy. She had blue eyes that turned up at the sides the way they would if you had your hair pulled really tight in a ponytail. She was very beautiful and intelligent.

One of the times when Jean and I broke up he took her to Culebra near Puerto Rico. I was so devastated that I could not get out of bed. Valda was involved with Jean on and off for years. Valda and I became friends even when I was with Jean. We liked each other very much and never felt jealous. Valda later told me that when she was in Culebra for two weeks with Jean that all he could do was talk about me. I loved Valda for this. That's the kind of girl she was. Sometimes, Valda, Jean and me would hang out together.

After Jean's death Valda took it upon herself to search for the child Jean had told her he had. Jean never told me this. However, he did tell several people that he got a girl pregnant in New Orleans on a one night stand and that the girl had the baby – a son named Noah. Valda told me that Jean often spoke to her of this child and that he was always sending money to the child's mother. Valda could never find the child.

I was once at the Great Jones loft and this gorgeous Black woman came over and asked Jean for abortion money. He took some money out of his sock and gave it to her.

After she left Jean asked me why I did not have his baby? I told him I could not have babies. He said that I was just saying that because I did not want to have his child. I just mumbled something back like, 'No, no. Maybe some other time . . .'

I never told Jean that the P.I.D. infection he gave to me had damaged me so badly. It would have hurt him so much to know and I am glad he never knew.

GOING TO THE FISH MARKET

After clubbing, at four in the morning, Suzanne and Jennifer take a taxi down to the fish market. Dressed in their black nightclub-dresses they walk among the barrels filled with fish. Their feet get caught in the wet nets on the ground. They listen to the fishermen boast and brag about their biggest catch and look into the dull, large eyes of dead fish.

Suzanne and Jennifer like to watch the sun rise. They like to examine the strange things that come out of the sea, accidentally caught in the nets: squid, crabs, a small shark, a yellow blouse, a turtle, an orange, oyster shells.

They don't talk about the clubs or the boys they met or did not meet. They don't talk about where they might be in ten years. They ooh and ahh over the shimmer of fish scales and talk and giggle with the fishermen.

One night after clubbing Jennifer and I went down to the docks to talk to the fishermen. This was something we did quite often. I remember one time someone had caught an enormous red and purple octopus. It lay inside a net. When we got up close to look, it suddenly let out a great stream of black ink that spattered all over our shoes.

SELLING
THE REFRIGERATOR

Suzanne calls Jennifer. She says she needs money to pay the rent. She has not paid the rent for five months. She is going to sell her refrigerator that is covered with Jean-Michel's doodles. Suzanne says that some representatives from Sotheby's already came over and agreed to auction it. Jennifer's boyfriend is a poet but he also has a trucking company called 'O'Neill Trucking'. Suzanne wants Jennifer's boyfriend to take the refrigerator to Christies.

The refrigerator sells for five thousand dollars. Andy Warhol buys it.

I was working as a waitress at Mike's American Grill. Each night after I finished waitressing I would call a limousine and drive around looking for Jean. I would go to the clubs or to his loft. Sometimes he would let me in and sometimes he wouldn't. I was really a mess. And really high on heroin. I had no shame whatsoever. I'm very embarrassed about it. I could not control myself. It was like I didn't care how I appeared. I was always very fabulous though. I had a lot of style and was very dramatic. Soon I stopped doing this. The limousines were so expensive that I didn't pay my rent. It was around this time that I sold my refrigerator at Sotheby's for five thousand dollars. I was nuts. I was obsessive. Then I realized I just had to get on with my life. I stopped stalking him and I just tried my very best to ignore the impulses. I stopped going to art galleries, I stopped hanging out with the people Jean and I knew together. I was trying to heal myself. It took everything I had inside to stop this behavior. But I did.

Then I got a job at Hawaii 5.0. and once in a while Jean would come by and stare in the window. He would not say anything and just stare and eventually he would leave. It reminded me of the way he used to stare at me at Night Birds when I first met him.

Sometimes he would come in with people like Lauren Hutton, Malcolm McLaren and others. He would stare at me with a mean look on his face. It was a small restaurant with only one small room so I was the only waitress and I would have to wait on them.

Jean loved to order me around. He would say, 'Waitress, would you dump my ashtray,' or 'Waitress, fill our water glasses.'

One day he came by and was just staring in the window so I went outside and asked him what he thought he was doing.

He said, 'I'm watching you, Venus – just watching you. Why don't you come over later?'

I said, 'No!' And then he grabbed my arms and said that he missed me.

I went to see him about one week later. He was so famous now that everything between us was very strained. People called him from all over the world and everyone was telling him how great he was. It was very sad because he did not seem to enjoy it at all. For example, Jean would be on the telephone talking to some German art dealer and then he'd get off the phone and go into the bathroom and vomit because of the drugs. Or an art critic would come by, drink some good wine, and go on and on about Jean's place in the art world. Jean would walk behind the guy and stick out his tongue. Jean hated art critics, he called them 'maggots'.

I left after a week and I don't think I ever slept with him again. It was too painful because by this time he could only think about heroin. I went to visit him and I went to dinner and parties with him but I never slept with him again. Then slowly, slowly I cut him out of my life completely.

THE LAST TIME SHE CALLS

The last time she calls up Jean-Michel on the telephone is when Andy Warhol dies.

She says, 'Jean, Jean, I am so sorry about Andy. How are you? Do you want me to come over?'

Jean says, 'No.' His voice is slurred and Suzanne can tell that he is very high on dope.

Suzanne keeps insisting, 'Should I come over? Do you want me to come?'

'Come and give me a bath, Venus,' he says.

'O.K. Jean.' she says. 'I'll be right over.'

When she gets to the loft Shenge opens the door. 'Go home, Suzanne' Shenge says. 'He is asleep, um, and dope-sick. Go home.'

Suzanne kisses Shenge's hand.

'Yes, yes,' she says.

I called Jean when Andy died. I knew he would be very upset. But he could hardly speak to me he was so out of it. In a slurred, whisper he kept asking me, 'what fables do you know?'

RUBY DESIRE

Suzanne changes her name to Ruby Desire. She has a big cowboy belt made that has a big brass buckle that says 'RUBY D.' The buckle is so large and heavy it looks like it could tip her over with its weight. It makes her walk leaning her body slightly to the left. She cannot run or skip anymore.

She sings, 'Do, re, mi, fa. Do, re, mi, fa,' over and over again until it becomes her own private language.

When people stop her on the street and say, 'Hi, Suzanne,' she answers, 'I am no longer Suzanne, I am Ruby Desire. Do, re, mi, fa.'

I decided that I wanted to sing. So I started taking voice lessons with a Jazz singer. I went three times a week. I saved up all my money and went into a little studio with an engineer and produced and made a demo tape.

I booked myself a show at Area and hired two big black bodyguards and a sax player. Everyone came. I sang two or three songs. I think I was probably really bad. But at least the hype was good. I had my hair done up like Priscilla Presley in the 60's and it took a lot of guts.

I made the bodyguards follow me around everywhere and light my cigarettes for me. I called myself Ruby Desire. I looked all over town for a red limousine but couldn't find one. So I knew all these East Village guys that drove old 60's classic motorbikes. A whole pack of them came with me and the leader had a red motorbike so I drove with him but with a scarf over my head so as not to ruin my hairdo. It was great. I sang 'Fever' and another song that was very poor that I wrote myself.

After singing I mingled with the crowd and my bodyguards followed me around everywhere. I heard someone say, 'Who the hell does she think she is with those bodyguards'. It was really a lot of hype. I put myself out there and was surprised at how good I was at promoting myself.

At this time I didn't talk to Jean at all. I wanted to be famous for myself and not as his girl.

I did other shows at Madame Rosa's and I started to really become known as Ruby Desire. To myself, though, the whole thing made me laugh. I never took any of it very seriously.

Around this time I met Jonathan Hood who was a singer and a songwriter. He really liked my voice and wanted to work with me. We started seeing each other and he soon moved into my apartment. I barely knew him. He was signed to Crepuscle Records based in Belgium. Jonathan was able to convince the record company to do a remake of Donna Summer's 'Bad Girls'. This record got a lot of club play in New York and I *started doing shows all over the place. Jonathan and I also started doing shows together as 'Ruby Desire and the Hood'.*

We did one really big show in the Michael Todd Room at the Palladium. I had two beautiful Black girls dancing behind me. We also had two bodyguards standing at the front of the stage wearing mirrored sun glasses. It was a really important show and it was very professional. By now I was pretty good and more relaxed and I was still studying voice.

Jonathan was friends with Mark Kamins, who was a big record producer. He came over to my apartment one day to play John something new he was working on. He just had the music down. It was sort of an African chant on top of a house beat. Jonathan convinced Mark to let me do the song and I wrote the lyrics for it.

The day I was recording the song, in walks this six foot five inch Rasta from Guyana with dread locks to his waist and tribal scars on his face. He was quite intimidating. His name was Warren Doris. It turned out that the song was his and he did the African chant or chorus on the song. The song turned out so well that within one month I was signed, along with Warren, to Capital Records.

Soon the song was released on a compilation album called The Black Havana Dance Compilation. *It had nine other new artists on it.*

As soon as the album came out it started going up the dance charts in America and England. Warren and I were sent on a tour to Europe with three other artists for one month and a half.

As I was the only white person on the tour, Warren protected me as best he could. He was into 'santeria' and made me wear magic beads under my costume and he would sprinkle me with holy water before we went on stage.

The whole experience was a nightmare even though we found out that the album had gone to number five on the dance charts in America and to number one in England. It was also the first time that I had been clean from alcohol and drugs for so many weeks.

After that tour I decided that I hated the music business and so I quit.

RUBY DESIRE PUTS AWAY HER COWBOY BELT

When Suzanne returns from Europe she puts her cowboy belt away at the back of her closet. New York feels different. She doesn't want to be who she was. She thinks it is because she needs some heroin. She thinks she needs to see Jean-Michel. She also needs a job.

When people on the street call out to her, 'Hello Ruby!' she answers, 'I am not Ruby anymore. I am Suzanne.'

She buys pink ballet shoes and wears them tied up her calf like a ballerina. She dyes her hair blue-black and cuts it short around her ears.

She goes to see Jean-Michel at the Great Jones loft. He lets her in.

He says, 'I always let you in, Venus.'

He is so thin he seems transparent. He stumbles when he walks and fans himself constantly with his hands. His teeth are covered with a yellowish film of dirt. His long arms are dry and covered with needle tracks. There is paint on his face and in his hair and sores on his cheeks.

*   *   *

He says, 'Why have you left me, Venus?'

Suzanne soothes him, caresses his hands, sucks his fingers and says, 'Things change, Jean. I have never left you.'

'Everyone has left me,' he says.

'Let me give you a bath,' Suzanne says. 'You always like that.'

She takes him to the bathroom, undresses him and puts him in the tub. She washes his hair and scrubs his skin being very careful not to hurt his sore arms. This is a body she no longer knows. She thinks he looks like a starved, ten year old child. She rubs his clavicle bones and his hip bones.

'You have to get clean, Jean,' she says. 'You have to just stop it.'

'I always loved it that you were the one person who never said that to me,' he answers. 'I'm sick and tired of people telling me to get off drugs.'

'I am sorry, Jean. I won't say it again,' the girl answers.

Jean-Michel lets Suzanne brush his teeth. He opens his mouth wide and says, 'Ahhhhhh.'

When I got back from Europe, which had been hell, I immediately went to see Jean. He was a mess and so I bathed him like I always used to. His paintings were all facing the wall so that he would not have to look at them. It was very strange. The only one I saw was Riddle Me This Batman *that was against the wall of the bathroom. In the center of the painting Jean had written, "NOTHING TO BE GAINED HERE." Further down in the painting he had written, "COWARDS WILL GIVE TO GET RID OF YOU."*

It was the first time I had ever seen him feeling sorry for himself. He was usually so gutsy.

After the bath we watched television and went to sleep. When I woke up he had already left the loft. He had left me a note that said, I remember it perfectly, 'Venus, morning glory, sweet potato, I have the money and you have the gold. JMB.'

Later I saw those words 'morning glory and sweet potato' in a painting of his, EROICA I, *one of his last paintings. On that same painting he had also written, 'man dies' four times.*

HE WAKES HER UP

One night Suzanne is asleep alone in her apartment and the doorbell rings. It is Jean-Michel. He asks if he can come in. Suzanne presses the buzzer and waits for him to come upstairs. She waits two minutes, three minutes, ten minutes and he doesn't appear.

Suzanne laces up her ballet shoes and runs downstairs but she can't find him. She walks around the block but she can't find him.

She is wide awake now and takes a taxi to buy some dope. On the way back to her apartment she asks the driver to go past the Great Jones loft. All the lights are turned off there and she goes home.

In her apartment Suzanne sniffs the heroin and her room looks round and blue. Words come to her mind in a great rush: Euclid, Newton, Galileo. She wants to look into microscopes and be surrounded by formulas and equations. She thinks about *Grey's Anatomy* and how she and Jean-Michel, high on coke, used to look at the book for hours as if they were reading a book on magic.

Suzanne remembers how Jean-Michel would paint and suddenly yell out to her, 'Venus, read me the names of the bones in an arm.' And she would call back, 'humerus, ulna, radius, carpus.'

Two weeks before his death, at two a.m., he came and rang my buzzer. I let him in but he never came up. He was in a very bad state and sounded desperate. But this was as much as he could do. He had crossed the line, the invisible line in drug addiction. Every heroin addict has some sense of where that line is. It is a choice to cross it. I chose not to.

I know that he came to say goodbye and this is the kindest thing he ever did for me. I know he came to say goodbye because he knew his death was imminent but then he must have suddenly changed his mind. He didn't want me to see him in such a terrible state, ravaged by heroin.

THE WEIGHT OF ARMS

Suzanne gets a job as a bartender at Tunnel. She works there five nights a week. This pays her rent and gives her enough money to buy heroin everyday. She sniffs it before work, during work and when she gets home. It has turned her into a skeleton with great big black holes for eyes. The heroin keeps her warm and safe. It is animal fur around her bones.

On August 12th, 1988 Jean-Michel is found dead from an overdose of heroin. He is found leaning in front of a fan as if he were trying to get some air to breath. It is determined that he choked on his vomit. No church agrees to perform the funeral service because Jean-Michel was not a member of any church. Finally the Frank E. Campbell Funeral Chapel agrees to hold the service. This is the place where all the jazz artists' funerals had been held.

I don't remember much about this time. I remember I rode over to the Great Jones loft on my bicycle just as Jean was being carried outside to the ambulance. I leaned against a wall covered in yellow graffiti that said, 'LISTEN, WATCH, MOON', and watched the shape of his body covered by a sheet being placed into the ambulance. I watched until the ambulance was out of sight. His body looked so small and flat under that sheet as if no one were really there.

I remember Rammellzee telling me that, 'The mutherfucker is dead!' I remember Rene Ricard saying, his teeth chattering, 'You are a widow now.' And, I remember calling Jean's father and asking him if I could go to the funeral because it was going to be a private funeral.

The casket was closed because he was so destroyed by heroin and because an autopsy had been performed.

My left arm weighed two pounds and my right arm weighed six pounds. I wanted to cover my mouth. Over and over I'd place my hand over my mouth. I knew that if I covered my mouth the knowledge of Jean's death could not get inside of me. It took two weeks before I could stop doing this.

Now, whenever I am around the Great Jones loft I will do anything not to walk near it. I cross the street or go around the block.

Even after all these years people are always looking for me. Strangers call me up. Dealers, collectors and biographers call me up. They all want to know what it was like to be with Jean. Sometimes I tell them. But they never get it right. I walk the places he has been.

SUZANNE

Suzanne covers her mouth with her hands. Over and over again, with quick bird-like gestures, she covers her mouth. She sleeps with a piece of cotton cloth over her lips. There are no teeth inside her words: AAAAAAAAAAAAAAAA.

Suzanne's heroin addiction lasted until late 1988. For several years she did volunteer work with drug addicts at Bernstein Drug Rehab and at Beth Israel Hospital and chaired her own NA meetings there. She also went back to high school and then on to college where she was a pre-med student. Suzanne is now in medical school doing her specialty in pediatrics.